PENGUIN BOOKS

THE NEW PENGUIN FREUD
GENERAL EDITOR: ADAM PHILLIPS

Civilization and Its Discontents

Sigmund Freud was born in 1856 in Moravia; between the ages of four and eighty-two his home was in Vienna: in 1938 Hitler's invasion of Austria forced him to seek asylum in London, where he died in the following year. His career began with several years of brilliant work on the anatomy and physiology of the nervous system. He was almost thirty when, after a period of study under Charcot in Paris, his interests first turned to psychology; and after ten years of clinical work in Vienna (at first in collaboration with Breuer, an older colleague) he invented what was to become psychoanalysis. This began simply as a method of treating neurotic patients through talking, but it quickly grew into an accumulation of knowledge about the workings of the mind in general. Freud was thus able to demonstrate the development of the sexual instinct in childhood and, largely on the basis of an examination of dreams, arrived at his fundamental discovery of the unconscious forces that influence our everyday thoughts and actions. Freud's life was uneventful, but his ideas have shaped not only many specialist disciplines, but also the whole intellectual climate of the twentieth century.

David McLintock studied comparative philology, historical linguistics and medieval literature at Oxford, Münster and Munich. He published extensively in these fields while teaching successively at the universities of Oxford, London and Cambridge, before turning to translation. He has translated numerous works of fiction, history and art history. He was awarded an Austrian state prize for translation in 1986 and the Schlegel-Tieck Prize in 1990 and 1996.

Leo Bersani was for many years Chair of the French Department at the University of California at Berkeley. His books include *The Freudian Body* (1986), *The Culture of Redemption* (1990), *Homos* (1995) and, in collaboration with Ulysse Dutoit, *Arts of Impoverishment: Beckett, Rothko, Resnais* (1994) and *Caravaggio's Secrets* (1998).

Adam Phillips was formerly Principal Child Psychotherapist at Charing Cross Hospital in London. He is the author of several books on psychoanalysis including *On Kissing, Tickling and Being Bored, Darwin's Worms, Promises, Promises* and *Houdini's Box*.

SIGMUND FREUD
Civilization and Its Discontents

Translated by David McLintock
with an Introduction by Leo Bersani

PENGUIN BOOKS

PENGUIN BOOKS

Published by the Penguin Group
Penguin Books Ltd, 80 Strand, London WC2R ORL, England
Penguin Putnam Inc., 375 Hudson Street, New York, New York 10014, USA
Penguin Books Australia Ltd, 250 Camberwell Road, Camberwell, Victoria 3124, Australia
Penguin Books Canada Ltd, 10 Alcorn Avenue, Toronto, Ontario, Canada M4V 3B2
Penguin Books India (P) Ltd, 11 Community Centre, Panchsheel Park, New Delhi – 110 017, India
Penguin Books (NZ) Ltd, Cnr Rosedale and Airborne Roads, Albany, Auckland, New Zealand
Penguin Books (South Africa) (Pty) Ltd, 24 Sturdee Avenue, Rosebank 2196, South Africa

Penguin Books Ltd, Registered Offices: 80 Strand, London WC2R ORL, England

www.penguin.com

Das Unbehagen in der Kultur first published 1930 (Leipzig, Vienna and Zürich:
Internationaler Psychoanalytischer Verlag)
'Die "Kulturelle" Sexualmoral und die moderne Nervosität' first published 1908 in
Sexual-Probleme 4 (3)
This translation published in Penguin Classics 2002

022

Sigmund Freud's German texts collected in *Gesammelte Werke* (1940–52)
copyright © Imago Publishing Co., Ltd, London, 1941, 1948
Translation and editorial matter copyright © David McLintock, 2002
Introduction copyright © Leo Bersani, 2002
All rights reserved

The moral rights of the translator and author of the Introduction have been asserted

Set in 10/12.5 pt PostScript Adobe New Caledonia
Typeset by Rowland Phototypesetting Ltd, Bury St Edmunds, Suffolk
Printed in England by Clays Ltd, St Ives plc

ISBN-13: 978–0–141–18236–0

www.greenpenguin.co.uk

Contents

Introduction

The incompatibility of civilization and individual happiness is at once a banality and an over-statement. Everyone knows that in order to enjoy the benefits of living in civilized groups we must all sacrifice, to some degree, the satisfaction of personal interests and passions. Not only that: civilization – to utter another commonplace – actually helps to create the conditions for happiness. As Freud recognizes in *Civilization and Its Discontents*, 'it is certain that all the means we use in our attempts to protect ourselves against the threat of suffering belong to this very civilization' to which he none the less assigns 'much of the blame for our misery' (pp. 25, 24). In any case, it might justifiably be thought that the tensions between the claims of the individual and those of civilization constitute an argument more appropriate to sociology than to psychoanalysis. Indeed, the argument is impressively elaborated in the work of the great sociologist Georg Simmel who, in his 1910 essay 'The Sociology of Sociability', formulated a thesis similar to Freud's in more measured, less melodramatic terms:

The great problems placed before [the ethical forces of society as it is] are that the individual has to fit himself into a whole system and live for it: that, however, out of this system values and enhancement must flow back to him, that the life of the individual is but a means for the ends of the whole, the life of the whole but an instrument for the purposes of the individual.

For Simmel, as, it would seem, for Freud, 'the great problem of association [of human groups]' is 'that of the measure of significance and accent which belongs to the individual as such in and as against the social milieu'.[1]

In referring to the sociological banality of *Civilization and Its Discontents'* thesis, I take my cue from Freud himself. One of the most curious aspects of *Civilization and Its Discontents* is Freud's reiterated self-reproach to the effect that he is not speaking psychoanalytically. The work was written in 1929, late in Freud's career, so it's not as if he hadn't had time to develop a distinctively psychoanalytic language. You would think that by now Freud would be 'speaking psychoanalysis' fluently. But the complaints start in Section III, where he laments that 'our study . . . has so far taught us little that is not generally known' (p. 24), little, that is, that might not have been said without the help of psychoanalysis. Given the repetition of this complaint three more times in the work, we should be alert to anything that breaks the self-critical trend, to any moment when Freud might be saying: 'This is it! Now I'm being profound, saying things that people didn't know before I said them! Now I'm speaking the language of psychoanalysis!'

To the reader's great relief, there is just such a moment in *Civilization and Its Discontents*. Before focusing on the crucial passage in which, apparently, Freud's investigation finally takes a distinctively psychoanalytic turn, let's note that the argument about human misery necessarily depends on certain assumptions about what would make us happy. While *Civilization and Its Discontents* will singularly complicate the very distinction between happiness and misery, twenty years earlier, in the essay '"Civilized" Sexual Morality and Modern Nervous Illness', Freud had offered a very *un*complicated version of the presumed opposition between civilization and individual happiness. In the 1908 piece, Freud doesn't worry about saying things that everyone already knows, and his argument is immediately recognizable as a psychoanalytic argument – if only in the crudest popular sense of what constitutes a psychoanalytic discourse. It's all about sex – just as the early critics of psychoanalysis complained. 'Anyone qualified to investigate the conditioning factors of nervous illness will soon be convinced that the increase of nervous disorders in our society is due to the greater restrictions placed on sexual activity' (p. 96). Or: 'the baleful influence of civiliz-ation is reduced to the harmful suppression of sexual life in civilized peoples (or classes) by the "civilized" sexual morality prevailing in them' (p. 88).

Freud anticipates the sexual liberationists of the 1960s, although he of course sounds more proper then they will even when he is making the most radical argument. Indeed, we shouldn't allow the propriety of vocabulary to obscure just how radical the argument is. Not only does civilization keep us from getting enough sex; it pre-vents us from having the kind of sex many of us most deeply want. 'Today's "civilized" sexual morality' permits 'only legitimate reproduction . . . as a sexual aim' (p. 92); it 'demands of the indi-vidual, whether man or woman . . . premarital abstinence, and life-long abstinence for all who do not enter into a lawful marriage' (p. 95). Since, as Freud had already argued in *Three Essays on the Theory of Sexuality* (1905), 'the human sex drive does not originally serve the purposes of reproduction at all', but rather aims 'to obtain particular kinds of pleasure', and since 'whole classes of individuals' don't quite make it 'from auto-eroticism to object-love, with the aim of genital union' (the presumably normative development), a monogamous heterosexual marriage is hardly a blueprint for univer-sal happiness. The sex life of individuals whose sexual development has been arrested can in fact 'take on a serviceable final form', and the sex drive of 'inverts' (homosexuals) even has 'a special aptitude', Freud claims, 'for cultural sublimation' (p. 92). But neither inverts nor other perverts can fully display their cultural gifts, since they have to suppress their drives without, however, being able to get rid of them. The 'perverse impulses', once repressed, come back in the disguise of neurotic symptoms: potentially healthy and socially viable sex drives have been transformed by 'civilized morality' into cul-turally useless nervous illness. Not only that: the developmentally lucky ones – heterosexual men and women with a predominantly genital sex drive – are not much happier than repressed perverts. Premarital abstinence leads people to seek 'a substitutive satisfaction of a neurotic kind, marked by pathological symptoms' (p. 96). Not only does it lead vast numbers of unhappy heterosexuals to expect much more, and more durable, sexual satisfaction than a monogamous union can bring; the frustrated male who has had recourse to masturbation and even homosexuality is also likely to have only 'limited potency' in marriage, which in turn makes it likely that his wife – already crippled by the sexual ignorance at least theoretically mandatory for proper young women in Freud's time – will be frigid. Thus 'preparation for marriage frustrates the aims of marriage itself' (p. 99); the disappointed couple 'will soon abandon sexual intercourse as the source of all their embarrassments, and with it the basis of married life' (p. 102).

'"Civilized" Sexual Morality and Modern Nervous Illness' is an eloquent indictment of a repressive sexual morality. While much of it seems dated today – especially the section on the enforced sexual ignorance of unmarried young women – it would be presumptuous to congratulate ourselves on having moved significantly beyond the sexual education of young people in the Vienna of Freud's lifetime. The American Christian right has successfully seen to it that a large number of sex education courses in high school 'teach' only abstinence and make no mention of contraception. Freud's essay is more a psychological curiosity than an historically obsolete document. For one thing, Freud seems astonishingly naive about the benefits of sex (lots of sex), even though, as we shall see, it is also Freud who has taught us to recognize his hymn of praise to sex as naive. Sexual abstinence (while it may be useful for 'young scholars . . .'), far from producing great artists or 'independent men of action or original thinkers, bold liberators and reformers', will 'more often . . . produce well-behaved weaklings who later merge into the great mass of those who habitually, if reluctantly, follow the lead given by strong [that is, strongly sexed?] individuals' (p. 98). Because women are denied 'the opportunity to take an intellectual interest in sexual problems . . . they are deterred from thinking at all, and knowledge loses its value for them'. The 'undoubted intellectual inferiority of so many women can be traced back to the inhibition of thought that is essential for sexual suppression' (p. 100). The energy with which a man pursues *all* his goals in life, Freud astonishingly and unquestioningly maintains, is a function of how 'energetically [he] conquers his sex object'. For 'a person's sexual behaviour often *sets the pattern* for all his other ways of reacting to the world' (p. 99).

Finally, Freud is extremely – and almost embarrassingly – ambiguous about all those 'substitutive' activities into which pre-marital abstinence pushes young people. On the one hand, they are emotionally and morally dangerous. Masturbation 'corrupts the character through *indulgence* in more ways than one' (masturbators will take 'the easy route' in the pursuit of 'significant goals'). Non-genital intercourse (the 'perverse' forms of sex – presumably oral and anal) 'are ethically objectionable in that they degrade a love-relationship between two human beings from something serious [that is, genital?] into a convenient game that entails no danger or spiritual involvement'. Perhaps most disastrously of all, constitutionally or developmentally predestined homosexuals 'are now joined by many others', who, unable to go along with 'the mainstream of the libido', glide into a considerably widened 'homosexual side-channel' (pp. 100–101). Worst of all – the argument is worth returning to – 'all those men who as a result of masturbatory or perverse practices have oriented their libido to anything other than the normal situations and conditions of satisfaction, develop a diminished potency in marriage' (p. 101). But why? You *might* argue that when 'normal' sex is finally allowed, potency would be increased: all that pent-up genitality can at last, legitimately and joyfully, explode. In '"Civilized" Sexual Morality and Modern Nervous Illness', Freud comes close to giving an anticipatory validation to homophobic fears, all too familiar to us, that heterosexuals can somehow be seduced into homosexuality and, especially, that if they do cross that line they may be permanently lost to, or spoiled for, heterosexuality. The normal, it would appear, is exceedingly vulnerable. To re-taste the perverse is to lose some of our passion for the non-perverse; the danger of developmental back-tracking is that we may never again have much enthusiasm for going forward.

'"Civilized" Sexual Morality and Modern Nervous Illness' is *psychoanalytically* muddled. By that I mean that its muddlement is constitutive of its limited but real interest. A rational and humane protest against the sexual abstinence imposed on sexually energetic young men and women is in fact a cry of alarm from someone who clearly – but also confusedly and perhaps unwillingly – knows something that this repressive society doesn't know (or pretends not to know). What he knows has something to do with both the power and the nature of sexuality. The apparent naiveté I referred to earlier about the benefits of lots of sex may be, more profoundly, a warning about the danger of postponing the pleasures of 'normal' intercourse. More exactly, it is a warning about the danger of postponing the repressive strength of those pleasures. Society's repression defeats a more important repression (important *for* society): a repression of *the sexual as such*. For if we need frequent sex, and if having sex makes us fit for all of life's other activities, it's because sex is something like – to use an image we will find in *Civilization and Its Discontents* – an oceanic force, one that threatens to flood our lives, to drown our other interests. The immense stupidity of society is to create the ideal conditions for such a flooding – that is, to liberate sexuality through the repression of sex. If society would just allow young men and women to have (presumably) normal sex, the women will think more clearly and the men will be better artists and bolder political activists. But by interfering with the teleology, the purpose and the direction of sexual development, society undoes one of the great conquests of human evolution: the use of reproductive sex as a sexual hygiene, a mode of sexual containment. The real substitutive activity is heterosexual genital monogamy; its milder pleasures discipline the overwhelming pleasures of perverse sex – which is to say, perhaps, the pleasures of the sexual itself. Astonishingly, then, Freud may secretly agree with the society he sternly criticizes: civilization requires sexual repression because unrepressed sexuality might destroy civilization. But *strategically* society has got it all wrong. The right way to go about the necessary damming up of the oceanic is to let people swim in the calmer waters of what might be called genital relationality: the waters of sex-cum-love, of sex promoted to, as Freud puts it, 'something serious', something more than mere 'indulgence', something 'that entails . . . danger or spiritual involvement' (p. 101). In other words, a kind of sublimated sexuality in which what is (necessarily?) repressed would no longer produce neurosis (that is, the inevitable return of the repressed in the disguise of neurotic symptoms).

Twenty years later, *Civilization and Its Discontents* will take up the principal thesis of ' "Civilized" Sexual Morality and Modern Nervous Illness', but the implicit optimism of the 1908 essay will be notably absent. Now there is hardly any suggestion that to remove the socially imposed barriers to sexual satisfaction would serve the cause of either civilization or individual happiness. For one thing, what a more liberal society might allow us to enjoy – non-monogamous heterosexual genital sex – is explicitly presented as a pale substitute for pleasures that *no* civilized society could be imagined as authorizing. In section II, Freud tells us that the intensity of satisfactions provided by scientific or artistic work is 'restrained when compared with that which results from the sating of crude, primary drives: they do not convulse our physical constitution' (p. 18). What did convulse our being, Freud suggests in the astonishing footnotes on the first and last pages of section IV, was the experience, or rather the smell of sex before we adopted an erect posture. But our sexuality fell when we stood up. Both anal eroticism and olfactory stimulation were subjected to what Freud calls 'organic repression' (p. 42); the result of this 'repression' is our horror of excrement and, at least according to Freud, a repugnance at sex, a shame provoked in us by our genitals and a disgust at genital odours which is so strong in many people that it 'spoil[s] their enjoyment of sexual intercourse'. And what a loss this was! By the end of the last footnote in section IV, Freud has transformed man's depreciation of the sense of smell in sex into the repression of 'the whole of his sexuality' (p. 43). Nothing is stranger in *Civilization and Its Discontents* than the erotically confessional footnotes – that is, those moments when the distinguished (if at times both extravagant and banal) anthropological imagination of the text descends into a footnote where it enjoys the fantasy of a mythic, prehistoric convulsing of our physical being in the passionate sniffing of a male on all fours.

An unfortunate consequence of evolution is, then, what most of us, according to Freud, experience as the 'unaccountable repugnance' (p. 43) that accompanies sexual love ('the model for all happiness', p. 37). At bottom, we are all insatiable and unhappily repressed perverts. We are, both ontogenetically and phylogenetically, 'coded' for pleasures we can no longer legitimately enjoy. But *Civilization and Its Discontents* goes even further than this. Not only is our sexuality dysfunctional from both developmental and evolutionary perspectives; there is, it would seem, something inherently dysfunctional in sexuality itself (repressed or unrepressed). At the the end of section IV, Freud raises a disturbing possibility: 'Now and then one seems to realize that this [the diminished importance of sex as a source of happiness] is not just the pressure of civilization, but that something inherent in the [sexual] function itself denies us total satisfaction and forces us on to other paths. This may be wrong – it is hard to decide' (p. 41). Wrong or not, this speculation governs the rest of *Civilization and Its Discontents*. In the footnote quoted from a moment ago and to which this sentence refers us, Freud is already trying to define that unsatisfactory something in the nature of sexuality itself. He comes up with three factors: the organic repression of our sense of smell and of anal eroticism (this is the conjecture 'that goes deepest'), our inherent bisexuality (which means, he writes, that the same object is not likely to satisfy both our male and female desires) and finally that 'degree of direct aggression' with which 'erotic relations are so often associated . . . quite apart from the sadistic component that properly belongs to them' (p. 43).

Thus begins the reflection on aggression – the real and profound subject of *Civilization and Its Discontents*, a subject which, from section V to VIII, will be promoted to the upper body of the text. To use the image from Romain Rolland which Freud has analysed in section I, aggression is the oceanic element that will flood the text of *Civilization and Its Discontents* – with, however, a crucial distinction. If the footnotes play the role of the psychoanalytic unconscious in this work, the material of the footnotes will be allowed into the text proper – into the quite proper text – only if its sexual components are expunged. And so, enacting compositionally his own formulation of the laws of repression and symptom-formation, Freud will devote the rest of his symptomatic upper text to the analysis of a presumably non-erotic aggression. Nowhere is the troubled speculative mobility of *Civilization and Its Discontents* more evident than in Freud's ultimately failed attempt to maintain the distinction between sexuality and aggression. The text's 'official' version of the aggressive drive is that it 'is the descendant and principal representative of the death drive, which we have found beside Eros and which rules the world jointly with him'. The reference is of course to the thesis of *Beyond the Pleasure Principle* (1920), and as in that work Freud maintains here 'the ubiquity of non-erotic aggression and destruction', at the same time that he recognizes, once again, that the death drive, from which that destruction derives, 'mostly eludes our perception, of course unless it is tinged with eroticism'. But now Freud goes further: 'Yet even where it appears without any sexual purpose, in the blindest destructive fury, there is no mistaking the fact that its satisfaction is linked with an extraordinarily high degree of narcissistic enjoyment, in that this satisfaction shows the ego how its old wish for omnipotence can be fulfilled' (p. 57).

Aggression is beginning to sound bizarrely like – of all things – the oceanic feeling, which Freud, correcting the religious emphasis given to that feeling by Romain Rolland, had defined as an ecstatic breaking down of the boundaries between the ego and the world traceable to the 'unlimited narcissism' of infancy. Like the oceanic feeling, aggressiveness includes an intense erotic pleasure. Against the view that the oceanic feeling is the source of religious sentiments, Freud had argued that it is probably rather 'an initial attempt at religious consolation', a delusionary cure for human suffering (p. 10). Now, however, Freud is suggesting that we suffer because civilization insists that we curb the 'extraordinarily high degree of narcissistic enjoyment' that accompanies satisfied aggression (that is, the successful breaking down of the world's resistances to, or more fundamentally, differences from, the ego). The oceanic feeling is the cure that religion proposes for the suffering caused by the curbing of the oceanic feeling – which is to say that the proposed cure for the illness is an idealized repetition of its origin. The oceanic feeling is a benign reformulation of 'the blindest destructive fury' (p. 57).

This mystification, however, points to a hidden truth about destructiveness: it is identical with love. Not only had Freud spoken, in the final footnote to section IV, of 'a degree of direct aggression' so often associated with erotic relations; not only does he recognize, as we have just seen, the intense narcissistic pleasure of destructiveness; he had even gone so far as to assert in section V, in objecting to the communists' argument that private property created aggression, that the latter 'forms the basis of all affectionate and loving relations among human beings, with perhaps the one exception of the relation between the mother and her male child' (p. 50). If we abolished the family and instituted complete sexual freedom, the indestructible destructiveness of human beings would still be with us. Only a few pages after Freud's very tentative suggestion at the end of section IV that 'something inherent in the [sexual] function itself' (p. 41) *may* prevent complete sexual happiness, he claims, without any tentativeness at all (even while continuing to insist on the non-erotic character of this aggressiveness), that an aggressive destructiveness 'forms the basis of' (p. 50) human love – which, I suggest, may be another way of saying that *destructiveness is constitutive of sexuality*. The explicit argument of *Civilization and Its Discontents* goes like this: we must sacrifice part of our sexuality and sublimate it into brotherly love in order to control our murderous impulses towards others. But the text obliquely yet insistently reformulates this argument in the following way: human love is something like an oceanic aggressiveness which threatens to shatter civilization in the wake of its own shattering narcissistic pleasure. We don't move *from* love *to* aggression in *Civilization and Its Discontents*; rather, love is redefined, re-presented, *as* aggressiveness.

Not only that: civilization itself repeats, rather than opposes, the other two terms, thereby transforming the argument of Freud's work into a triple tautology: sexuality = aggression = civilization. It is by no means certain that civilization can maintain itself as a distinct term within what might be called the oceanic textuality of *Civilization and Its Discontents*, a textuality that breaks down the boundaries separating concepts. I referred at the beginning of this discussion to Freud's dissatisfaction, expressed several times in *Civilization and Its Discontents*, with the ordinariness of his own ideas. He claims to be painfully aware of discovering nothing, in this investigation, 'that is not generally known' (p. 24) It is only in the middle of section VII that Freud finally announces an idea worthy of a new science, a new way of thinking about the human mind. 'And here at last an idea comes in that belongs entirely to psychoanalysis and is foreign to our ordinary way of thinking.' What is that idea? It tells us, Freud continues, that while 'it is at first the conscience . . . that causes us to renounce the drives, this causal relation is later reversed. Every renunciation of the drives now becomes a dynamic source of conscience; every fresh renunciation reinforces its severity and intolerance.' And Freud declares himself 'tempted to endorse the paradoxical statement that conscience results from [rather than is the cause of] the renunciation of the drives' (p. 65). It would seem, then, that paradox is central to psychoanalytic thinking. There is, however, something troubling in the fact that *Civilization and Its Discontents* has been dealing in paradoxes long before Freud announced the arrival of an idea worthy of psychoanalysis. We have learned, for example, that the more virtuous a man is the more severe is his super-ego, and that he blames himself for misfortunes for which he is clearly not responsible. Such paradoxes may be at first puzzling, but they are resolvable. To renounce satisfaction of a drive is not to renounce the desire associated with the drive; the frustration of a desire increases its intensity, and so saints, Freud remarks, are not so wrong to call themselves sinners: frustrated temptations are inescapable temptations.

Freud moves on, however, to say something quite different: renunciation itself *produces* conscience. The more familiar view, Freud reminds us, is that 'the original aggression of the conscience continues the severity of the external authority and has therefore nothing to do with renunciation' (p. 65). But internalization turns out to have two very different aspects. On the one hand, the authority becomes an internal watch-dog and is thereby able to continue to exercise its prohibitive functions. Civilization thus inhibits aggression by sending it back where it came from; conscience, or the super-ego, treats the ego with the same harsh aggressiveness that the ego would like to direct towards others. On the other hand, Freud tells us, external authority – civilization and its representatives – is internalized *in order to be attacked*. The authority's imagined aggression toward the desiring subject is taken over by the subject, not only to discipline desire but also in order to attack the authority itself. The subject-ego is being punished for its guilty desires, but the punishing energy is taken from the subject's fury at the agent of punishment, who in fact also becomes its object. The child is showing the father what a good punishing father he, the child, would be, but since it is aggression towards the father which allows for this instructive demonstration, the object of it is bound to be the father, 'degraded', as Freud says, to sitting in for or as the child in the punished ego. This ferociously severe conscience is already present within the renounced instinctual drives. We no longer have the paradox of virtue intensifying the reproaches of conscience, a paradox explained, and dissolved, by the role of secret desires compensating for the renounced behaviour. Now we are not speaking of degrees of guilt or of moral severity but rather of an aggressiveness that accompanies renounced desire. The external authority's severe demands on the subject are fused with the subject's vengeful anger at those demands, both of which constitute the subject's renunciation: the consequence, and the content, of renunciation are a doubly reinforced conscience.

What has happened to civilization? More pertinently, *what is civilization*? What does it mean to say that civilization inhibits aggression or to assert, as Freud does in his concluding section, that 'the sense of guilt [is] the most important problem in the development of civilization and the price we pay for cultural progress is a loss of happiness, arising from a heightened sense of guilt' (p. 71)? The text has by now made a quite different argument: the renunciation of aggression is inherent in its constitution. But it is a renunciation that multiplies the force of aggression. In giving up the satisfaction of a drive, we simultaneously: (1) internalize the authority presumably inhibiting the drive, (2) increase our sense of guilt by intensifying our desire for satisfaction, (3) submit the ego to the fury of an aggressiveness originally intended for the inhibiting external authority. Given the limitations of our effective power over the external world, it could be said that the curbing of aggressiveness offers the only realistic strategy for satisfying aggressiveness. And the inhibiting power of what Freud calls civilization is unintelligible – if we exclude the crudest exercise of power, in which people are physically subjected to the will of others – except in terms of those internal mechanisms that I have just outlined. In a very important sense, civilization in Freud, at least that aspect of it which he thinks of as a socialized super-ego, is merely a cultural metaphor for the psychic fulfilment in each of us of a narcissistically thrilling wish to destroy the world, a wish 'fulfilled' in a monstrously ingenious phantasmatic scenario of self-destruction. From this perspective, civilization is not the tireless if generally defeated opponent of individual aggressiveness; rather, it is the *cause* of the very antagonism that *Civilization and Its Discontents* sets out to examine. The regulator of aggression is identical to the very problem of aggression.

We have moved very far indeed from an optimistic view of sexuality's beneficent influence on the individual as well as on civilization. A more liberal sexual ethic would, Freud suggested in ' "Civilized" Sexual Morality and Modern Nervous Illness', make individuals happier, help to preserve the institution of marriage, and free the mental energy indispensable to artistic and scientific achievement. This is a psychoanalytic programme closer to Wilhelm Reich than to Freud; it is psychoanalysis in the service of a gospel of sexual liberation. For the Freud of *Civilization and Its Discontents*, sexuality is certainly as important as it was in 1908, but there has been a momentous shift of perspective: now sexuality is the ineradicable, intractable source of our *un*happiness. And this view implies a distinction – absent from the earlier essay – between sex and sexuality. In the first few sections of *Civilization and Its Discontents*, Freud seems to be talking about certain kinds of *behaviour* that would make the individual happy but that civilization prohibits. By the end of section IV, we are dealing with something quite different.

Not only is the behaviour that would make us happy a monstrous anomaly (remember that pre-historic sniffing male on all fours), but now we are being asked to look at a psychic 'function', at something like a fundamental psychic posture towards the world. We may, with Freud, call that posture sexuality, but it has very little to do with sex. We may, also with Freud, wish to call it aggression, but this is an aggression of enormous erotic power, an aggression that may even be constitutive of sexuality.

It should at once be said that this blurring of distinctions is by no means what Freud the rational thinker *wants*. Indeed, the opposition advanced in *Beyond the Pleasure Principle* between Eros and Thanatos (between, on the one hand, sexuality, and on the other, aggression and a death drive) – an opposition that Freud unreservedly reasserts in *Civilization and Its Discontents* – might even be thought of as an anticipatory theoretical defence against the *collapse* of that very dualism into a nearly inconceivable sameness. Freud resolutely holds on to the notion of a non-erotic aggression at the same time that his argument moves inexorably towards a view of aggression (directed towards the world or towards the self) *as* intense erotic excitement. The latter view is the language of psychoanalysis, although it is a language at odds with what language usually does. It abolishes the differences and spaces that separate terms and concepts; it transforms oppositions into repetitions, and threatens to reduce discourse to a numbing display of redundancies. This is not to say that such redundancies cover all of reality. Psychoanalysis is not about all of reality; it treats, properly, 'only' sexuality (and its detractors are right about this), but the sexuality it treats is a kind of vast tautology within the human psyche, one to which what we call the sexual act is nearly irrelevant. Psychoanalysis teaches us to recognize that tautology as an always imminent threat to our negotiations with the differences and the non-redundant spaces of the authentically non-erotic real.[2]

In terms of a particular life's history, the psychic posture just described accounts for *our never losing anything*. In psychoanalysis, nothing is ever forgotten, given up, left behind. In section I of *Civilization and Its Discontents*, Freud claims that 'in mental life, nothing that has once taken shape can be lost', and, soon after this, 'everything past survives' (pp. 7, 9). Everything persists; psychoanalysis classifies the modalities of persistence and return: conscious memory, slips-of-the-tongue, repression, symptomatic behaviour, acting out, sublimation. *Civilization and Its Discontents* textually confirms this law. It wanders, and Freud appears to have trouble finding his subject (the function of religion, the conditions of happiness, the nature of civilization, erotic and non-erotic drives, the aetiology of conscience). And yet aggressiveness comes to include everything: it is accompanied by an intense erotic pleasure; like the oceanic feeling discussed in section I, it breaks down the boundaries between the self and the world; it gives expression both to instinctual needs and, in the form of conscience, to the inhibiting energy of civilization. Psychoanalysis does not deny the world's existence, but it does document the procedures by which the mind de-materializes the world, absorbs it into a history of fantasy-representations. To complain, for example, as critics have done, that Freud turned away from the real world and studied the seduction of children only as fantasy is like complaining about astronomers turning their analytic attention to the stars. Psychoanalysts are no more and no less capable than anyone else of recognizing such phenomena as real child abuse, but that recognition is irrelevant to what is 'psychoanalytic' in psychoanalysis. It may not, however, be irrelevant to suggest the very limited usefulness of psychoanalysis in describing, or training us for, what I called a moment ago our negotiations with the non-erotic real. Lacan's assaults on ego psychology can be best justified as a profound fidelity to psychoanalysis itself, as a recognition that a psychology of adaptation to the world is by definition a non-psychoanalytic psychology. Psychoanalysis gives a persuasive account not of human adjustment but of that which makes us unfit for civilized life. This should at the very least cast some doubt on the validity of *any* notion of a psychoanalytic 'cure'. The clinical practice of psychoanalysis is grounded in a theory that tells us why we can't be cured. The 'illness' in question takes on great anecdotal variety in individual lives (and this naturally provides ample material for clinical work), but our blind destructive fury is an intractable psychic function, and positioning in the world, rather than a deviation from some (imaginary) psychic normality. We can, at best (as long as we remain within psychoanalysis), adapt to that which makes us incapable of adaptation. To go any further (again, within psycho-analysis) would be to cure ourselves of being human.

Leo Bersani, 2001

Notes

1. Georg Simmel, 'The Sociology of Sociability', in *On Individuality and Social Forms*, ed. Donald N. Levine (Chicago: University of Chicago Press, 1971), pp. 137 and 130.
2. Ulysse Dutoit and I attempt to show what such exchanges with the world might be like (sensual exchanges that at once acknowledge and dismiss the erotic) in both *Arts of Impoverishment: Beckett, Rothko, Resnais* (Cambridge, MA: Harvard University Press, 1994) and *Caravaggio's Secrets* (Cambridge, MA: MIT Press, 1998).

Translator's Preface

Sigmund Freud wrote an elegant, cultivated and largely unprofessorial German and so won himself a readership that extended far beyond narrow academic circles. In this respect he may be compared with Friedrich Nietzsche, who couched his ideas in a powerful, rhythmical prose that appealed to an educated public long before his academic colleagues in Germany began to take him seriously as a philosopher. The comparison is of course inexact: the two had very different styles of writing, and while Freud soon attracted an academic following, which went on increasing until and beyond his death, Nietzsche's grew more slowly and was subject to shifts in the political climate.

A translator naturally wishes to reproduce the effect that the author's text has had on readers of the original. Having previously translated novels and works on history and art history, I knew that most readers would be unfamiliar with the original language and therefore unlikely to question the accuracy of the rendering. Yet in the case of Freud's writings I knew I must never forget that they have the status of 'canonical texts'. By allowing myself the slightest licence I might well mistranslate an important term. English-speaking Freudians may know little or no German, but they can always refer to the Standard Edition and compare the use of certain terms with what they find in a new translation. If there are discrepancies, it follows that one of the translators has falsified the sense, and it will not take long to discover which of the two is guilty, for they are unlikely to conclude that the Master failed to make himself clear.

Psychoanalysis, a Viennese growth, was first described and discussed in German. However, it has for decades been practised in

English-speaking countries and written about in English, and as a result an English psychoanalytic vocabulary has been built up by anglophone practitioners and translators. It is clear that if we were now starting from scratch we might choose different renderings of a number of terms, but in most cases we have little choice left. Being an outsider, I am most concerned about Freudian uses that do violence to what I consider normal English and are apt to displease the general reader. As an example I will take the rendering of the German pair *Lust/Unlust* by 'pleasure/unpleasure'. In English we have 'pain' and 'displeasure' as antonyms of 'pleasure', but neither of these is appropriate in a Freudian context – although Freud often uses *Schmerz* ('pain') in close proximity to *Unlust*. As for 'unpleasure', the *Oxford English Dictionary* (2nd edn, 1989, XIX, p. 143) cites uses of the word by Fanny Burney and Coleridge and defines it as 'unpleasantness; (something that causes) displeasure'; the psychoanalytic usage is defined as 'the sense of inner pain, discomfort, or anxiety which results from the blocking of an instinctual impulse by the ego and is the opposite of the affect of pleasure'. Hence, 'unpleasure' seems to be rare and obsolete except in psychoanalytic parlance, where it is an awkward part-by-part rendering of the German *Unlust*. On the other hand, English has the serviceable adjectival pair 'pleasurable/unpleasurable'; I have therefore preferred to render the German pair *Lust/Unlust* by 'pleasurable experience/unpleasurable experience', or some such.

Often discussed, but to little purpose, is the rendering of the key terms *das Ich*, *das Es* and *das Über-Ich*, all of which are made up of German elements and would be translated literally as 'the I', 'the it' and 'the over-I'. Their established English equivalents are 'the ego', 'the id' and 'the super-ego'. It has been objected that, since German makes do with native words, the English translator should not resort to Latin. However, this is to ignore not only the different histories of the two languages (in forming new words, German relies much more on native resources than English does on its Anglo-Saxon heritage), but certain parallels that link them. It is worth noting that in German and English the substantivized pronouns *das Ich* and 'the ego' (as well as 'the self' – I think, for instance, that the German

Ichgefühl is best translated by 'sense of self') were in use long before Freud, and that in compounds the German prefix *Über-* corresponds regularly to 'super-'. The new coinages *das Es* and 'the id' fitted in well with the pre-existent phrases *das Ich* and 'the ego' at a time when most English readers had a modicum of Latin (though they may have had no German).

Freud's original title for his last major work was *Das Unglück in der Kultur* ('Unhappiness in Civilization'). He later replaced *Unglück* by *Unbehagen* ('unease, *malaise*, discomfort'), and the title he suggested to Joan Riviere, his translator, was 'Man's Discomfort in Civilization'. She, however, chose to reverse the order of the nouns, change the syntactic relation between them, and render *Unbehagen* by 'discontents', this last choice having perhaps been suggested by Freud's use of *Unzufriedenheit* ('dissatisfaction, discontent') in association with *Unbehagen* at one point in the last section of the work (*ein Unbehagen, eine Unzufriedenheit*: 'an unease, a discontent').

They concurred in using 'civilization' and 'civilized', rather than 'culture' and 'cultural', to render *Kultur* and *kulturell*. Translated into English, the relevant senses of *Kultur*, as defined in *Der Grosse Duden*, the authoritative German dictionary, are (a) 'the totality of the intellectual, artistic and creative achievements of a community as an expression of human progress' and (b) 'the totality of the characteristic intellectual, artistic and creative achievements produced by a particular community in a particular region during a particular period', for example 'Greek culture', 'monastic culture', 'the culture of the Italian Renaissance', 'working-class culture', etc.

In the *OED* (2nd edn, IV, p. 121) *culture* is defined as (a) 'the training, development, and refinement of mind, tastes, and manners; the condition of being thus trained and refined; the intellectual side of civilization' and (b) 'a particular form or type of intellectual development', also as 'the civilization, customs, artistic achievements, etc. of a people, esp. at a certain stage of its development or history'. *Civilization* is defined (III, p. 257) as 'civilized condition or state; a developed or advanced state of human society; a particular stage or a particular type of this'; its opposite being sometimes 'barbarism' or 'barbarity'. Among the collocations cited are 'Egyptian civilization', 'the civilization of Europe', 'the ancient civilizations'. It is clear, then, that the meanings of the English words overlap and that either might have been chosen as an equivalent of the German word. No doubt 'civilization' was preferred because it was the more inclusive term, involving more than mind, taste and manners.

One problem that faced English-speaking psychoanalysts was the translation of the German word *Trieb*, long established in common usage (in the sense of 'impulse') and in philosophical discourse. When Mozart's *Le Nozze di Figaro* is sung in German, Cherubino addresses those who know *die Triebe des Herzens* ('the impulses of the heart'), and Friedrich Schiller invented the notion of the *Spieltrieb*, now known to us as the 'play drive'. From the *OED* (IV, p. 1060) we learn that in the journal *Mind* XIII, p. 165 (1888) it was stated that *Trieb* had 'no good single equivalent in English'. By 1918 the German psychological sense began to be transferred to the pre-existent English word 'drive', which corresponds etymologically almost exactly to the German word. The *OED* defines this new sense of the English word as (a) 'any internal mechanism which sets an organism moving or sustains its activity in a certain direction, or causes it to pursue a certain satisfaction; a motive principle; any tendency to persistent behaviour directed at a goal; esp. one of the recognized physiological tensions or conditions of need, such as hunger and thirst'; (b) 'any type of persistent behaviour or disposition that would lead to the attainment of a certain goal'. The German word derives from the verb *treiben* ('to drive, to impel'), and so an obvious rendering would be 'impulse', but impulses tend to be momentary, not persistent. Freudians at first translated *Trieb* by 'instinct', the relevant senses of which are defined in the *OED* (VII, pp. 1044f.) as 'innate impulse; natural or spontaneous tendency or inclination' and 'an innate propensity in organized beings (esp. in the lower animals), varying with the species, manifesting itself in acts which appear to be rational, but are performed without conscious design or intentional adaptation of means to ends'. This was obviously unsatisfactory, if only because the 'organized beings' in question were human beings, commonly credited with superior rationality. The derivative adjective *triebhaft* was rendered, not by the established word 'instinctive', current since the seventeenth century, but by the recent derivative 'instinctual', first attested in 1924 and absent from the first edition of the *OED* (1933). At first, then, *Trieb* and *triebhaft* were paralleled by the English pair 'instinct/instinctual', whose first member was subsequently replaced by 'drive', so that now, until a derivative of 'drive' is invented, we shall have to make do with the unmatching pair 'drive/instinctual'.

Freudians will of course continue to read Freud's works either in German or in the English of the Standard Edition. I hope, however, that my versions will make these twentieth-century classics marginally more accessible to the readers of the twenty-first century.

Civilization and Its
Discontents

I

It is impossible to resist the impression that people commonly apply false standards, seeking power, success and wealth for themselves and admiring them in others, while underrating what is truly valuable in life. Yet in passing such a general judgement one is in danger of forgetting the rich variety of the human world and its mental life. There are some individuals who are venerated by their contemporaries, but whose greatness rests on qualities and achievements that are quite foreign to the aims and ideals of the many. One may be inclined to suppose that these great men are appreciated after all only by a minority, while the great majority have no interest in them. However, it is probably not as simple as that, owing to the discrepancies between people's thoughts and actions and the diversity of their desires.

One of these outstanding men corresponds with me and in his letters calls himself my friend. I sent him a little piece of mine that treats religion as an illusion, and in his reply he said that he wholly agreed with my view of religion, but regretted that I had failed to appreciate the real source of religiosity. This was a particular feeling of which he himself was never free, which he had found confirmed by many others and which he assumed was shared by millions, a feeling that he was inclined to call a sense of 'eternity', a feeling of something limitless, unbounded – as it were 'oceanic'. This feeling was a purely subjective fact, not an article of faith; no assurance of personal immortality attached to it, but it was the source of the religious energy that was seized upon by the various churches and religious systems, directed into particular channels and certainly consumed by them. On the basis of this oceanic feeling alone one was entitled to call oneself religious, even if one rejected every belief and every illusion.

This opinion of my esteemed friend, who himself once celebrated the magic of illusion in poetic form, caused me no small difficulty.[1] I can discover no trace of this 'oceanic' feeling in myself. It is not easy to treat feelings scientifically. One may try to describe their physiological symptoms. Where this is not feasible – and I fear that the oceanic feeling will not lend itself to such a description – there is nothing left to do but to concentrate on the ideational content most readily associated with the feeling. If I have understood my friend correctly, what he has in mind is the same as the consolation that an original and rather eccentric writer offers his hero before his freely chosen death: 'We cannot fall out of this world.'[2] It is a feeling, then, of being indissolubly bound up with and belonging to the whole of the world outside oneself. I would say that for me this is more in the nature of an intellectual insight, not of course without an emotional overtone, though this will be not be wanting in other acts of thought that are similar in scope. Relying on my personal experience, I should not be able to convince myself of the primary nature of such a feeling. But this does not entitle me to dispute its actual occurrence in others. The only question is whether it is correctly interpreted and whether it should be acknowledged as the *fons et origo* of all religious needs.

I have nothing to suggest that would decisively contribute to the solution of this problem. The idea that a person should be informed of his connection with the world around him through an immediate feeling that is used for this purpose from the beginning sounds so bizarre, and fits so badly into the fabric of our psychology, that we are justified in looking for a psychoanalytic – that is to say a genetic – derivation of such a feeling. The following train of thought then suggests itself. Normally we are sure of nothing so much as a sense of self, of our own ego. This ego appears to us autonomous, uniform and clearly set off against everything else. It was psychoanalytic research that first taught us that this was a delusion, that in fact the ego extends inwards, with no clear boundary, into an unconscious psychical entity that we call the id, and for which it serves, so to speak, as a façade. And psychoanalysis still has much to tell us about the relation of the ego to the id. Yet externally at least the ego seems to be clearly and sharply delineated. There is only one condition – admittedly an unusual one, though it cannot be dismissed as pathological – in which this is no longer so. At the height of erotic passion the borderline between ego and object is in danger of becoming blurred. Against all the evidence of the senses, the person in love asserts that 'I' and 'you' are one and is ready to behave as if this were so. What can be temporarily interrupted by a physiological function must of course be capable of being disturbed by morbid processes also. Pathology acquaints us with a great many conditions in which the boundary between the ego and the external world becomes uncertain or the borderlines are actually wrongly drawn. There are cases in which parts of a person's own body, indeed parts of his mental life – perceptions, thoughts, feelings – seem alien, divorced from the ego, and others in which he attributes to the external world what has clearly arisen in the ego and ought to be recognized by it. Hence, even the sense of self is subject to disturbances, and the limits of the self are not constant.

A further consideration tells us that the adult's sense of self cannot have been the same from the beginning. It must have undergone a process of development, which understandably cannot be demonstrated, though it can be reconstructed with a fair degree of probability.[3] The new-born child does not at first separate his ego from an outside world that is the source of the feelings flowing towards him. He gradually learns to do this, prompted by various stimuli. It must make the strongest impression on him that some sources of stimulation, which he will later recognize as his own physical organs, can convey sensations to him at any time, while other things – including what he most craves, his mother's breast – are temporarily removed from him and can be summoned back only by a cry for help. In this way the ego is for the first time confronted with an 'object', something that exists 'out there' and can be forced to manifest itself only through a particular action. A further incentive to detach the ego from the mass of sensations, and so to recognize a 'world outside', is provided by the frequent, multifarious and unavoidable feelings of pain (or absence of pleasure), whose termination and avoidance is required by the absolute pleasure principle. A tendency arises to detach from the ego anything that may give rise to such unpleasurable experience, to expel it and so create an ego that is oriented solely towards pleasure and confronts an alien and menacing world outside. The limits of this primitive pleasure-oriented ego are inevitably corrected by experience. After all, some of the things that give us pleasure and that we are loath to forgo belong not to the ego, but to the object, and some of the torments that we wish to expel prove to be of internal origin and inseparable from the ego. We learn how to distinguish between the internal, which belongs to the ego, and the external, which comes from the world outside, through deliberate control of our sensory activity and appropriate muscular action. This is the first step towards establishing the reality principle, which will govern subsequent developments. The distinction between the internal and the external naturally serves a practical purpose, in that it provides protection against unpleasurable experiences and the threat of them. The fact that the ego employs exactly the same methods to expel certain unpleasurable sensations from within as it does to repel others from without becomes the starting point for significant pathological disorders.

In this way, then, the ego detaches itself from the external world. Or, to put it more correctly, the ego is originally all-inclusive, but later it separates off an external world from itself. Our present sense of self is thus only a shrunken residue of a far more comprehensive, indeed all-embracing feeling, which corresponded to a more intimate bond between the ego and the world around it. If we may assume that this primary sense of self has survived, to a greater or lesser extent, in the mental life of many people, it would coexist, as a kind of counterpart, with the narrower, more sharply defined sense of self belonging to the years of maturity, and the ideational content appropriate to it would be precisely those notions of limitlessness and oneness with the universe – the very notions used by my friend to elucidate the 'oceanic' feeling. But have we any right to assume that what was originally present has survived beside what later evolved from it?

Undoubtedly! There is nothing surprising about such an occurrence, either in the mental sphere or in other spheres. Regarding the animal world, we adhere to the hypothesis that the most highly developed species have evolved from the lowest. Yet we find all the simple forms of life still existing today. The race of the great saurians has become extinct and made way for the mammals, but a genuine representative of this race, the crocodile, is still with us. The analogy may be too remote, and it is weakened by the fact that as a rule the lower species that survive are not the true ancestors of the more highly developed species of today. The intermediate stages have mostly died out and are known to us only through reconstructions. In the realm of the mind, however, the retention of the primitive beside what has evolved from it is so common that there is no need to cite examples to prove it. When this happens it is mostly the result of divergent developments. One portion (in quantitative terms) of an attitude, of an instinctual impulse, has remained unchanged, while another has developed further.

This brings us up against the more general problem of retention in the psychical sphere, which has so far hardly been studied, but is so fascinating and significant that we may perhaps be permitted, though not for any adequate reason, to dwell on it for a while. Having overcome the error of thinking that our frequent forgetfulness amounts to the destruction of the trace left by memory and therefore to an act of annihilation, we now tend towards the opposite presumption – that, in mental life, nothing that has once taken shape can be lost, that everything is somehow preserved and can be retrieved under the right circumstances – for instance, through a sufficiently long regression. Let us try to understand, with the help of an analogy from another field, what this presumption implies. As an example let us take the development of the Eternal City.[4] Historians tell us that in the earliest times Rome was *Roma quadrata*, an enclosed settlement on the Palatine Hill. The next phase was the *Septimontium*, a union of the settlements on the separate hills. After this it was the city bounded by the Servian Wall, and still later, after all the vicissitudes of the republican and the early imperial age, the city that the emperor Aurelian enclosed within his walls. We will not pursue the further transformations undergone by the city, but we cannot help wondering what traces of these early stages can still be found by a modern visitor to Rome – whom we will credit with the best historical and topographical knowledge. He will see Aurelian's wall virtually unchanged, save for a few gaps. Here and there he will find stretches of the Servian wall that have been revealed by excavations. Because he commands enough knowledge – more than today's archaeologists – to be able to trace the whole course of this wall and enter the outlines of *Roma quadrata* in a modern city plan. Of the buildings that once occupied this ancient framework he will find nothing, or only scant remains, for they no longer exist. An extensive knowledge of the Roman republic might at most enable him to say where the temples and public buildings of that period once stood. Their sites are now occupied by ruins – not of the original buildings, but of various buildings that replaced them after they burnt down or were destroyed. One need hardly add that all these remnants of ancient Rome appear as scattered fragments in the jumble of the great city that has grown up in recent centuries, since the Renaissance. True, much of the old is still there, but buried under modern buildings. This is how the past survives in historic places like Rome.

Now, let us make the fantastic assumption that Rome is not a place where people live, but a psychical entity with a similarly long, rich past, in which nothing that ever took shape has passed away, and in which all previous phases of development exist beside the most recent. For Rome this would mean that on the Palatine hill the imperial palaces and the Septizonium of Septimius Severus still rose to their original height, that the castle of San Angelo still bore on its battlements the fine statues that adorned it until the Gothic siege. Moreover, the temple of Jupiter Capitolinus would once more stand on the site of the Palazzo Caffarelli, without there being any need to dismantle the latter structure, and indeed the temple would be seen not only in its later form, which it assumed during the imperial age, but also in its earliest, when it still had Etruscan elements and was decorated with terracotta antefixes. And where the Coliseo now stands we could admire the vanished Domus Aurea of Nero; on the Piazza of the Pantheon we should find not only the present Pantheon, bequeathed by Hadrian, but the original structure of M. Agrippa; indeed, occupying the same ground would be the church of Maria sopra Minerva and the ancient temple over which it is built. And the observer would perhaps need only to shift his gaze or his position in order to see the one or the other.

It is clearly pointless to spin out this fantasy any further: the result would be unimaginable, indeed absurd. If we wish to represent a historical sequence in spatial terms, we can do so only by juxtaposition in space, for the same space cannot accommodate two different things. Our attempt to do otherwise seems like an idle game; its sole justification is to show how far we are from being able to illustrate the peculiarities of mental life by visual means.

There is one objection that we must try to answer. Why did we choose to compare the past of a city with the psychical past? Even where the life of the psyche is concerned, the assumption that everything past survives is valid only if the mind has remained intact and its fabric has not suffered from trauma or inflammation. However, destructive factors that might be compared with such causes of disease, are not absent from the history of any city, even if it has had a less turbulent past than Rome or, like London, hardly ever been ravaged by an enemy. Even the most peaceful urban development entails the demolition and replacement of buildings, and so for this reason no city can properly be compared with a psychical organism.

We readily yield to this objection and, forgoing any striking contrast, turn to a more closely related object of comparison, the animal or human body. But here too we find the same phenomena. The earlier phases of development are not preserved at all, having been absorbed into the later ones, for which they supplied the material. The embryo cannot be discovered in the adult; the thymus gland of the child is replaced after puberty by connective tissue, but no longer exists as such; in the adult's marrow-bone I can admittedly trace the outline of the child's bone, but this has disappeared through stretching and thickening before taking on its final form. The fact remains that the retention of all previous stages, together with the final shape, is possible only in the mind, and that we are not in a position to illustrate this phenomenon by means of any parallel.

Perhaps we go too far in making this assumption. Perhaps we should be content to say that the past *may* be retained in the life of the psyche and *need not* be destroyed. It may be that even in the psychical sphere some things that are old are so obscured or consumed – in the normal way of things, or in exceptional circumstances – that there is no longer any way of restoring and reviving them, or that their retention is linked to certain favourable conditions. This may be so, but we have no way of knowing. All we can do is hold on to the fact that in mental life the retention of the past is the rule, rather than a surprising exception.

Hence, if we are prepared to acknowledge that an 'oceanic' feeling exists in many human beings and inclined to trace it back to an early phase of the sense of self, a further question arises: what claim has this feeling to be regarded as the source of religious needs?

I do not find such a claim compelling. After all, a feeling can be a source of energy only if it is itself the expression of a strong need. To me the derivation of religious needs from the helplessness of the child and a longing for its father seems irrefutable, especially as this feeling is not only prolonged from the days of childhood, but constantly sustained by a fear of the superior power of fate. I cannot cite any childish need that is as strong as the need for paternal protection. The role of the oceanic feeling, which might seek to restore unlimited narcissism, is thus pushed out of the foreground. The origin of the religious temperament can be traced in clear outline to the child's feeling of helplessness. Something else may be concealed behind it, but for the time being this remains obscure.

I can imagine that the oceanic feeling subsequently became connected with religion. Being at one with the universe, which is the intellectual content associated with this feeling, strikes us as an initial attempt at religious consolation, as another way of denying the danger that the ego perceives as a threat from the outside world. I must confess yet again that I find it very hard to work with these almost intangible concepts. Another of my friends, whose insatiable thirst for knowledge has driven him to conduct the most extraordinary experiments and finally made him virtually omniscient, has assured me that in practising yoga one can actually arouse new sensations and universal feelings in oneself by turning away from the outside world, by fixing one's attention on bodily functions, and by breathing in special ways. Such sensations and feelings he would interpret as regressions to ancient conditions in the life of the psyche that have long been overlaid. He sees in them a physiological justification, so to speak, for much of the wisdom of mysticism. This would suggest connections with many obscure psychical states such as trance and ecstasy. Yet I cannot help exclaiming, with the diver in Schiller's ballad:

Es freue sich, wer da atmet im rosigen Licht.

[Let him rejoice, whoever draws breath in the roseate light!]

Notes

1. [*Addition 1931:*] *Liluli*, 1923 [1919]. – Since the appearance of *La Vie de Ramakrishna* [1929] and *La Vie de Vivekananda* (1930) I need no longer conceal the fact that the friend referred to above is Romain Rolland.
2. D. Chr. Grabbe, *Hannibal:* 'Ja, aus der Welt werden wir nicht fallen. Wir sind einmal darin [Yes, we shall not fall out of the world. We are in it once and for all].'
3. See the numerous works on the development of the ego and the sense of self, from Ferenczi, *Entwicklungsstufen des Wirklichkeitssinns* (1913) to the contributions of P. Federn 1926, 1927 and later.
4. This information is taken from *The Cambridge Ancient History*, part VII (1928), 'The Founding of Rome', by Hugh Last.

I I

In my piece entitled 'The Future of an Illusion' I was much less concerned with the most profound sources of religious sentiment than with what the common man understands by his religion, the system of teachings and promises that on the one hand explains to him, with enviable thoroughness, the riddles of this world, and on the other assures him that a careful providence will watch over his life and compensate him in a future existence for any privations he suffers in this. The common man cannot imagine this providence otherwise than as an immensely exalted father. Only such a being can know the needs of the children of men, be softened by their pleas and propitiated by signs of their remorse. All this is so patently infantile, so remote from reality, that it pains a philanthropic temperament to think that the great majority of mortals will never be able to rise above such a view of life. It is still more embarrassing to learn how many of those living today, who cannot help seeing that this religion is untenable, nevertheless seek to defend it, bit by bit, in pathetic rearguard actions. One would like to mingle with the believers, in order to confront those philosophers who think they can rescue the God of religion by replacing him with an impersonal, shadowy, abstract principle, and to remind them of the commandment: 'Thou shalt not take the name of the Lord thy God in vain.' If some of the greatest spirits of the past did the same, we cannot appeal to their example here, for we know why they had to.

Let us return to the common man and his religion, the only one that deserves the name. The first thing that occurs to us is the well-known remark by one of our great poets and thinkers, which describes how religion relates to art and science:

Wer Wissenschaft und Kunst besitzt,
hat auch Religion;
Wer jene beiden nicht besitzt,
der habe Religion![1]

[Whoever possesses science and art also has religion; whoever possesses neither of these, let him have religion!]

On the one hand these lines contrast religion with man's two highest achievements; on the other they state that, when it comes to the value they have in our lives, they can represent or stand in for one another. Even if we wish to deny the common man's claim to religion, we clearly lack the authority of the poet. We will try to get closer to an appreciation of his proposition by adopting a special approach. The life imposed on us is too hard for us to bear: it brings too much pain, too many disappointments, too many insoluble problems. If we are to endure it, we cannot do without palliative measures. (As Theodor Fontane told us, it is impossible without additional help.) Of such measures there are perhaps three kinds: powerful distractions, which cause us to make light of our misery, substitutive satisfactions, which diminish it, and intoxicants, which anaesthetize us to it. Something of this sort is indispensable.[2] Voltaire has distractions in mind when he ends his *Candide* with the advice that one should cultivate one's garden; another such distraction is scholarly activity. Substitutive satisfactions, such as art affords, are illusions that contrast with reality, but they are not, for this reason, any less effective psychically, thanks to the role that the imagination has assumed in mental life. Intoxicants affect our physical constitution and alter its chemistry. It is not easy to define the position that religion occupies in this series. We shall have to approach the matter from a greater distance.

The question of the purpose of human life has been posed innumerable times; it has not yet received a satisfactory answer and perhaps does not admit of one. Some of those who have posed it have added that if life should turn out to have no purpose, it would lose any value it had for them. Yet this threat alters nothing. Rather, it seems that one is entitled to dismiss the question. The threat appears to rest upon the very human presumption of which we have so many other instances. No one talks about the purpose of the life of animals, unless it is that they are meant to serve human beings. Yet this too is untenable, for there are many animals that man can do nothing with – except describe, classify and study them – and countless animal species have escaped even this use by living and dying out before man set eyes on them. Again, only religion has an answer to the question of the purpose of life. It can hardly be wrong to conclude that the notion that life has a purpose stands or falls with the religious system.

We will therefore turn now to the more modest question of what human beings themselves reveal, through their behaviour, about the aim and purpose of their lives, what they demand of life and wish to achieve in it. The answer can scarcely be in doubt: they strive for happiness, they want to become happy and remain so. This striving has two goals, one negative and one positive: on the one hand it aims at an absence of pain and unpleasurable experiences, on the other at strong feelings of pleasure. 'Happiness', in the strict sense of the word, relates only to the latter. In conformity with this dichotomy in its aims, human activity develops in two directions, according to whether it seeks to realize – mainly or even exclusively – the one or the other of these aims.

As we see, it is simply the programme of the pleasure principle that determines the purpose of life. This principle governs the functioning of our mental apparatus from the start; there can be no doubt about its efficacy, and yet its programme is at odds with the whole world – with the macrocosm as much as with the microcosm. It is quite incapable of being realized; all the institutions of the universe are opposed to it; one is inclined to say that the intention that man should be 'happy' has no part in the plan of 'creation'. What we call happiness, in the strictest sense of the word, arises from the fairly sudden satisfaction of pent-up needs. By its very nature it can be no more than an episodic phenomenon. Any pro-longation of a situation desired by the pleasure principle produces only a feeling of lukewarm comfort; we are so constituted that we can gain intense pleasure only from the contrast, and only very little from the condition itself.[3] Hence, our prospects of happiness are already restricted by our constitution. Unhappiness is much less difficult to experience. Suffering threatens us from three sides: from our own body, which, being doomed to decay and dissolution, cannot dispense with pain and anxiety as warning signals; from the external world, which can unleash overwhelming, implacable, destructive forces against us; and finally from our relations with others. The suffering that arises from this last source perhaps causes us more pain than any other; we are inclined to regard it as a somewhat superfluous extra, though it is probably no less ineluctable than suffering that originates elsewhere.

It is no wonder that, under the pressure of these possibilities of suffering, people are used to tempering their claim to happiness, just as the pleasure principle itself has been transformed, under the influence of the external world, into the more modest 'reality principle'; that one counts oneself lucky to have escaped unhappiness and survived suffering; and that in general the task of avoiding suffering pushes that of obtaining pleasure into the background. Reflection teaches us that we can try to perform this task by following very different paths; all these paths have been recommended by various schools of worldly wisdom and trodden by human beings. Unrestricted satisfaction of all our needs presents itself as the most enticing way to conduct one's life, but it means putting enjoyment before caution, and that soon brings its own punishment. The other methods, which aim chiefly at the avoidance of unpleasurable experience, differ according to which source of such experience is accorded most attention. Some of them are extreme and others moderate; some are one-sided, and some tackle the problem at several points simultaneously. Deliberate isolation, keeping others at arm's length, affords the most obvious protection against any suffering arising from interpersonal relations. One sees that the happiness that can be attained in this way is the happiness that comes from peace and quiet. Against the dreaded external world one can defend onself only by somehow turning away from it, if one wants to solve the problem unaided. There is of course another, better path: as a member of the human community one can go on the attack against nature with the help of applied science, and subject her to the human will. One is then working with everyone for the happiness of all. The most interesting methods of preventing suffering are those that seek to influence one's own constitution. Ultimately, all suffering is merely feeling; it exists only in so far as we feel it, and we feel it only because our constitution is regulated in certain ways.

The crudest, but also the most effective method of influencing our constitution is the chemical one – intoxication. No one, I think, fully understands how it works, but it is a fact that there are exogenous substances whose presence in the blood and tissues causes us direct feelings of pleasure, but also alters the determinants of our sensibility in such a way that we are no longer susceptible to unpleasurable sensations. Both effects not only occur simultaneously: they also seem closely linked. However, there must also be substances in the chemistry of our bodies that act in a similar way, for we know of at least one morbid condition – mania – in which a condition similar to intoxication occurs, without the introduction of any intoxicant. Moreover, in our normal mental life there are oscillations between fairly easy releases of pleasure and others that are harder to come by, and these run parallel to a lesser or a greater susceptibility to unpleasurable feelings. It is much to be regretted that this toxic aspect of mental processes has so far escaped scientific investigation. The effect of intoxicants in the struggle for happiness and in keeping misery at a distance is seen as so great a boon that not only individuals, but whole nations, have accorded them a firm place in the economy of the libido. We owe to them not only a direct yield of pleasure, but a fervently desired degree of independence from the external world. We know, after all, that by 'drowning our sorrows' we can escape at any time from the pressure of reality and find refuge in a world of our own that affords us better conditions for our sensibility. It is well known that precisely this property of intoxicants makes them dangerous and harmful. In some circumstances they are responsible for the futile loss of large amounts of energy that might have been used to improve the lot of mankind.

The complicated structure of our mental apparatus, however,

admits of a good many other influences too. Just as the satisfaction of the drives spells happiness, so it is a cause of great suffering if the external world forces us to go without and refuses to satisfy our needs. One can therefore hope to free oneself of part of one's suffering by influencing these instinctual impulses. This kind of defence against suffering is no longer brought to bear upon the sensory apparatus; it seeks to control the inner sources of our needs. In extreme cases this is done by stifling the drives in the manner prescribed by the wisdom of the east and put into effect in the practice of yoga. If it succeeds, one has admittedly given up all other activity too – indeed, sacrificed one's life – only to arrive, by a different route, at the happiness that comes from peace and quiet. We follow the same route when our aims are less extreme and we seek merely to *control* our drives. Control is then exercised by the higher psychical authorities, which have subjected themselves to the reality principle. At the same time the aim of satisfaction is by no means abandoned; a certain protection against suffering is obtained, in that failure to satisfy the drives causes less pain if they are kept in thrall than if they are wholly uninhibited. All the same, the possibilities of pleasure are undeniably diminished. The feeling of happiness resulting from the satisfaction of a wild instinctual impulse that has not been tamed by the ego is incomparably more intense than that occasioned by the sating of one that has been tamed. Here we have an economic explanation for the irresistibility of perverse impulses, perhaps for the attraction of whatever is forbidden.

Another technique for avoiding suffering makes use of the displacements of the libido that are permitted by our psychical apparatus and lend its functioning so much flexibility. Here the task is to displace the aims of the drives in such a way that they cannot be frustrated by the external world. Sublimation of the drives plays a part in this. We achieve most if we can sufficiently heighten the pleasure derived from mental and intellectual work. Fate can then do little to harm us. This kind of satisfaction – the artist's joy in creating, in fashioning forth the products of his imagination, or the scientist's in solving problems and discovering truths – has a special quality that it will undoubtedly be possible, one day, to describe in metapsychological terms. At present we can only say, figuratively, that they seem to us 'finer and higher', but their intensity is restrained when compared with that which results from the sating of crude, primary drives: they do not convulse our physical constitution. The weakness of this method, however, lies in the fact that it cannot be employed universally, as it is accessible only to the few. It presupposes special aptitudes and gifts that are not exactly common, not common enough to be effective. And even to the few it cannot afford complete protection against suffering; it does not supply them with an armour that is proof against the slings and arrows of fortune, and it habitually fails when one's own body becomes the source of the suffering.[4]

It is already clear, in the case of this last method, that the purpose is to make oneself independent of the external world by seeking satisfaction in internal, psychical processes, but in the next one the same features are brought out even more strongly. Here the link with reality is loosened still further; satisfaction is derived from illusions, which one recognizes as such without letting their deviation from reality interfere with one's enjoyment. The sphere in which these illusions originate is the life of the imagination, which at one time, when the sense of reality developed, was expressly exempted from the requirements of the reality test and remained destined to fulfil desires that were hard to realize. Foremost among the satisfactions we owe to the imagination is the enjoyment of works of art; this is made accessible, even to those who are not themselves creative, through the mediation of the artist.[5] It is impossible for anyone who is receptive to the influence of art to rate it too highly as a source of pleasure and consolation in life. Yet the mild narcosis that art induces in us can free us only temporarily from the hardships of life; it is not strong enough to make us forget real misery.

Another method, which operates more energetically and more thoroughly, sees reality as the sole enemy, the source of all suffering, something one cannot live with, and with which one must therefore sever all links if one wants to be happy, in any sense of the word. The hermit turns his back on the world and refuses to have anything to do with it. But one can do more than this: one can try to re-create the world, to build another in its place, one in which the most intolerable features are eliminated and replaced by others that accord with one's desires. As a rule anyone who takes this path to happiness, in a spirit of desperate rebellion, will achieve nothing. Reality is too strong for him. He will become a madman and will usually find nobody to help him realize his delusion. It is asserted, however, that in some way each of us behaves rather like a paranoiac, employing wishful thinking to correct some unendurable aspect of the world and introducing this delusion into reality. Of special importance is the case in which substantial numbers of people, acting in concert, try to assure themselves of happiness and protection against suffering through a delusional reshaping of reality. The religions of mankind too must be described as examples of mass delusion. Of course, no one who still shares a delusion will ever recognize it as such.

This is not, I think, a complete list of the methods that human beings employ in trying to gain happiness and keep suffering at bay, and I am aware that the material can be arranged differently. There is one method that I have not yet mentioned – not because I have forgotten it, but because it will concern us later in another context. How could one possibly forget this particular technique in the art of living? It is distinguished by the most curious mixture of characteristics. Naturally it seeks independence from what may best be called fate, and to this end it transfers satisfaction to internal mental processes and makes use of the facility for libidinal displacement that has already been mentioned. But it does not turn away from the external world: on the contrary, it clings to the things of this world and obtains happiness through an emotional attachment to them. Nor is it content with the avoidance of unpleasurable experience, a goal that derives, as it were, from tired resignation; indeed, it bypasses this goal, pays no attention to it, and adheres to the original, passionate striving for the positive achievement of happiness. Perhaps it actually gets closer to this goal than any other method. I am referring of course to the way of life that places love at the centre of everything and expects all satisfaction to come from loving and being loved. This kind of mental attitude comes naturally enough to us all; one manifestation of love, sexual love, has afforded us the most potent experience of overwhelming pleasure and thereby set a pattern for our quest for happiness. What is more natural than that we should go on seeking happiness on the path where we first encountered it? The weakness of this technique of living is obvious; if it were not, nobody would have thought of abandoning this route to happiness in favour of another. We never have so little protection against suffering as when we are in love; we are never so desolate as when we have lost the object of our love or its love for us. But this is not the last word on this particular technique of living, which is based on the value of love as a means of happiness: there is much more to be said about it.

Here one can bring in the interesting case in which happiness in life is sought mainly in the enjoyment of beauty, wherever it presents itself to our senses and our judgement – the beauty of human forms and gestures, of natural objects and landscapes, of artistic and even scientific creations. This aesthetic approach to the purpose of life affords little protection against the sufferings that threaten us, but it can make up for much. The enjoyment of beauty has a special quality of feeling that is mildly intoxicating. Beauty has no obvious use, nor is it easy to see why it is necessary to civilization; yet civilization would be unthinkable without it. The science of aesthetics investigates the conditions under which the beautiful is apprehended; it has not been able to clarify the nature and origin of beauty; as commonly happens, the absence of results is shrouded in a wealth of high-sounding, empty verbiage. Unfortunately psychoanalysis too has scarcely anything to say about beauty. All that seems certain is its origin in the sphere of sexual feeling; it would be an ideal example of an aim-inhibited impulse. 'Beauty' and 'attractiveness' are originally properties of the sexual object. It is notable that the genitals themselves, the sight of which is always exciting, are hardly ever judged beautiful; on the other hand, the quality of beauty seems to attach to certain secondary sexual characteristics.

Despite the incompleteness of my presentation, I venture to offer, even at this early stage, a few remarks to round off our present enquiry. The programme for attaining happiness, imposed on us by the pleasure principle, cannot be fully realized, but we must not – indeed cannot – abandon our efforts to bring its realization somehow closer. To reach this goal we may take very different routes and give priority to one or the other of two aims: the positive aim of gaining pleasure or the negative one of avoiding its opposite. On neither route can we attain all we desire. Happiness, in the reduced sense in which it is acknowledged to be possible, is a problem concerning the economy of the individual libido. There is no advice that would be beneficial to all; everyone must discover for himself how he can achieve salvation. The most varied factors will come into play and direct his choice. It is a question of how much real satisfaction he can expect from the external world, how far he is led to make himself independent of it, and, finally, how much strength he feels he has to change it in accordance with his wishes. Apart from the external conditions, what will be decisive here is the individual's mental constitution. The predominantly erotic person will give priority to his emotional relations with others; the narcissistic person, being more self-sufficient, will seek the most important satisfactions in his own internal mental processes; the man of action will not give up contact with the external world, on which he can test his strength. For the second of these types the nature of his gifts and the extent to which he is able to sublimate his drives will determine where he should lodge his interests. Any extreme decision will be penalized, in that it will expose the individual to the dangers that arise if he has chosen one technique of living to the exclusion of others. Just as the prudent merchant avoids tying up all his capital in one place, so worldly wisdom will perhaps advise us not to expect all our satisfaction to come from one endeavour. Success is never certain; it depends on the coincidence of many factors, and perhaps on none more than the capacity of our psychical constitution to adapt its functioning to the environment and to exploit the latter for the attainment of pleasure. Anyone who has been born with a particularly unfavourable instinctual constitution and who has not properly undergone the transformation and reordering of the components of his libido – a process that is indispensable for later achievements – will find it hard to derive happiness from his external situation, especially if he is faced with fairly difficult tasks. As a last technique for living, which at least promises him substitutive satisfactions, he may take refuge in neurotic illness; this usually happens early in life. Anyone who sees his quest for happiness frustrated in later years can still find consolation in the pleasure gained from chronic intoxication, or make a desperate attempt at rebellion and become psychotic.[6]

Religion interferes with this play of selection and adaptation by forcing on everyone indiscriminately its own path to the attainment of happiness and protection from suffering. Its technique consists in reducing the value of life and distorting the picture of the real world by means of delusion; and this presupposes the intimidation of the intelligence. At this price, by forcibly fixing human beings in a state of psychical infantilism and drawing them into a mass delusion, religion succeeds in saving many of them from individual neurosis. But it hardly does any more; there are, as we have said, many paths that can lead to such happiness as is within the reach of human beings, but none that is certain to do so. Not even religion can keep its promise. If the believer is finally obliged to speak of God's 'inscrutable decrees', he is admitting that all he has left to him, as the ultimate consolation and source of pleasure in the midst of suffering, is unconditional submission. And if he is ready to accept this he could probably have spared himself the detour.

Notes

1. Goethe, *Zahme Xenien* IX (*Gedichte aus dem Nachlass* [Poems published posthumously]).
2. On a more basic level Wilhelm Busch says the same in *Die Fromme Helene*: 'Wer Sorgen hat, hat auch Likör [Whoever has cares has liquor too].'
3. Goethe even reminds us:

> *Alles in der Welt lässt sich ertragen,*
> *Nur nicht eine Reihe von schönen Tagen.*

[Everything in the world can be endured, except a succession of fine days.]

However, this may be an exaggeration.

4. Unless a special aptitude dictates the direction that a person's interest in life is to take, the ordinary professional work available to everyone can occupy the place assigned to it by Voltaire's wise advice. Within the scope of a short survey it is not possible to pay sufficient attention to the vital role of work in the economy of the libido. No other technique for the conduct of life binds the individual so firmly to reality as an emphasis on work, which at least gives him a secure place in one area of reality, the human community. The possibility of shifting a large number of libidinal components – narcissistic, aggressive, even erotic – towards professional work and the human relations connected with it lends it a value that is in no way inferior to the indispensable part it plays in asserting and justifying a person's existence in society. Special satisfaction comes from professional activity when this is freely chosen and therefore makes possible the use, through sublimation, of existing inclinations, of continued or constitutionally reinforced instinctual impulses. And yet people show scant regard for work as a path to happiness. They do not strive after it as they do after other possibilities of satisfaction. The great majority work only because they have to, and this aversion to work is the source of the most difficult social problems.

5. Cf. 'Formulierungen über die zwei Prinzipien des psychischen Geschehens' ['Formulations on the Two Principles of Psychic Functioning'], 1911 (*Gesammelte Werke*, vol. VIII) and *Vorlesungen zur Einführung in die Psychoanalyse*, XXIII [*Introductory Lectures on Psycho-Analysis*] (*Gesammelte Werke*, vol. XI).

6. [*Addition 1931:*] I feel impelled to point out at least one of the gaps that have remained in the presentation given above. No consideration of the possibilities of human happiness should fail to take into account the relation between narcissism and object libido. We need to know what being essentially reliant on our own resources means for the economy of the libido.

III

Our study of happiness has so far taught us little that is not generally known. Even if we go on to ask why it is so difficult for people to be happy, the prospect of learning something new seems little better. We have already answered this question by pointing to the three sources of our suffering: the superior power of nature, the frailty of our bodies, and the inadequacy of the institutions that regulate people's relations with one another in the family, the state and society. Regarding the first two, our judgement cannot vacillate for long: it obliges us to acknowledge these sources of suffering and submit to the inevitable. We shall never wholly control nature; our constitution, itself part of this nature, will always remain a transient structure, with a limited capacity for adaptation and achievement. Recognition of this fact does not have a paralysing effect on us; on the contrary, it gives direction to our activity. Even if we cannot put an end to all suffering, we can remove or alleviate some of it; the experience of thousands of years has convinced us of this. Our attitude to the third source of suffering, the social source, is different. We refuse to recognize it at all; we cannot see why institutions that we ourselves have created should not protect and benefit us all. However, when we consider how unsuccessful we have been at preventing suffering in this very sphere, the suspicion arises that here too an element of unconquerable nature may be at work in the background – this time our own psyche.

When considering this possibility, we come up against a contention which is so astonishing that we will dwell on it for a while. It is contended that much of the blame for our misery lies with what we call our civilization, and that we should be far happier if we were to abandon it and revert to primitive conditions. I say this is astonishing because, however one defines the concept of civilization, it is certain that all the means we use in our attempts to protect ourselves against the threat of suffering belong to this very civilization.

By what route have so many people arrived at this strange attitude of hostility to civilization? I think a deep, long-standing dissatisfaction with the state of civilization at any given time prepared the ground on which a condemnation of it grew up owing to particular historical causes. I think I can identify the last two of these; I am not sufficiently erudite to trace the causal chain back far enough into the history of the human race. Some such hostility to civilization must have been involved already in the victory of Christianity over paganism. After all, this hostility was very close to the devaluation of earthly life that came about through Christian teaching. The penultimate cause arose when voyages of discovery brought us into contact with primitive peoples and tribes. Owing to inadequate observation and the misinterpretation of their manners and customs, they appeared to the Europeans to lead a simple, happy life, involving few needs, which was beyond the reach of their culturally superior visitors. Subsequent experience has corrected several such judgements; the fact that these peoples found life so much easier was mistakenly ascribed to the absence of complicated cultural requirements, when in fact it was due to nature's bounty and the ease with which their major needs could be satisfied. The final cause is particularly familiar to us; it arose when we became acquainted with the mechanism of the neuroses that threaten to undermine the modicum of happiness enjoyed by civilized man. It was discovered that people became neurotic because they could not endure the degree of privation that society imposed on them in the service of its cultural ideals, and it was inferred that a suspension or a substantial reduction of its demands would mean a return to possibilities of happiness.

There is an added factor of disappointment. In recent generations the human race has made extraordinary advances in the natural sciences and their technical application, and it has increased its control over nature in a way that would previously have been unimaginable. The details of these advances are generally known and need not be enumerated. Human beings are proud of these achievements, and rightly so. Yet they believe they have observed that this newly won mastery over space and time, this subjugation of the forces of nature – the fulfilment of an age-old longing – has not increased the amount of pleasure they can expect from life or made them feel any happier. We ought to be content to infer from this observation that power over nature is not the sole condition of human happiness, just as it is not the sole aim of cultural endeavours, rather than to conclude that technical progress is of no value in the economy of our happiness. By way of objection it might be asked whether it is not a positive addition to my pleasure, an unequivocal increment of my happiness, if I can hear, as often as I wish, the voice of the child who lives hundreds of miles away, or if a friend can inform me, shortly after reaching land, that he has survived his long and arduous voyage. Is it of no importance that medicine has succeeded in significantly reducing infant mortality and the risk of infection to women in childbirth, and in adding a good many years to the average life-span of civilized man? We can cite many such benefits that we owe to the much-despised era of scientific and technical advances. At this point, however, the voice of pessimistic criticism makes itself heard, reminding us that most of these satisfactions follow the pattern of the 'cheap pleasure' recommended in a certain joke, a pleasure that one can enjoy by sticking a bare leg out from under the covers on a cold winter's night, then pulling it back in. If there were no railway to overcome distances, my child would never have left his home town, and I should not need the telephone in order to hear his voice. If there were no sea travel, my friend would not have embarked on his voyage, and I should not need the telegraph service in order to allay my anxiety about him. What is the good of the reduction of infant mortality if it forces us to practise extreme restraint in the procreation of children, with the result that on the whole we rear no more children than we did before hygiene became all-important, but have imposed restraints on sexual life within marriage and probably worked against the benefits of natural selection? And finally, what good is a long life to us if it is hard, joyless and so full of suffering that we can only welcome death as a deliverer?

It seems certain that we do not feel comfortable in our present civilization, but it is very hard to form a judgement as to whether and to what extent people of an earlier age felt happier, and what part their cultural conditions played in the matter. We shall always tend to view misery objectively, that is to project ourselves, with all our demands and susceptibilities, into *their* conditions, and then try to determine what occasions for happiness or unhappiness we should find in them. This way of looking at things, which appears objective because it ignores the variations in subjective sensitivity, is of course the most subjective there can be, in that it substitutes our own mental state for all others, of which we know nothing. Happiness, however, is something altogether subjective. However much we recoil in horror when considering certain situations – that of the galley slave in ancient times, of the peasant in the Thirty Years War, of the victim of the Holy Inquisition, of the Jew waiting for the pogrom – it is none the less impossible for us to empathize with these people, to divine what changes the original insensitivity, the gradual diminution of sensitivity, the cessation of expectations, and cruder or more refined methods of narcotization have wrought in man's receptivity to pleasurable and unpleasurable feelings. In cases where there is a possibility of extreme suffering, certain protective psychical mechanisms are activated. It seems to me fruitless to pursue this aspect of the problem any further.

It is time to consider the essence of the civilization whose value for our happiness has been called into question. We will refrain from demanding a formula that captures this essence in a few words before we have learnt anything from our investigation. We will content ourselves with repeating[1] that the word 'civilization' designates the sum total of those achievements and institutions that distinguish our life from that of our animal ancestors and serve the dual purpose of protecting human beings against nature and regulating their mutual relations. In order to understand more, we will bring together the individual features of civilization as they manifest themselves in human communities. In doing so we have no hesitation in letting ourselves be guided by linguistic usage or, as some would say, a 'feeling for language', trusting that in this way we shall do justice to inner perceptions that still refuse to be expressed in abstract terms.

The first stage is easy: we recognize as belonging to civilization all activities and values that are useful to human beings, by making the earth serviceable to them, by protecting them against violent natural forces, and so forth. About this aspect of civilization there can be scarcely any doubt. If we go back far enough, we find that the first civilized activities were the use of tools, the taming of fire, and the building of dwellings. Among these, the taming of fire stands out as a quite extraordinary and unprecedented achievement;[2] with the others man struck out on paths that he has continued to follow ever since, the stimulus to which is not hard to guess. With all his tools man improves on his own organs, both motor and sensory, or clears away the barriers to their functioning. Engines place gigantic forces at his disposal, which he can direct, like his muscles, wherever he chooses; the ship and the aeroplane ensure that neither water nor air can hinder his movements. By means of spectacles he can correct the defects of his ocular lens; with the telescope he can see far into the distance; and with the microscope he can overcome the limits of visibility imposed by the structure of the retina. In the camera he has created an instrument that captures evanescent visual impressions, while the gramophone record does the same for equally fleeting auditory impressions; both are essentially materializations of his innate faculty of recall, of his memory. With the help of the telephone he can hear sounds from distances that even the fairy tale would respect as inaccessible. Writing is in origin the language of the absent, the house a substitute for the womb – one's first dwelling place, probably still longed for, where one was safe and felt so comfortable.

What man, through his science and technology, has produced in this world, where he first appeared as a frail animal organism and where every individual of his species must still make his entry as a helpless babe – 'oh inch of nature!' – all this not only sounds like a fairy tale, but actually fulfils all – no, most – fairy-tale wishes. All these assets he can claim as cultural acquisitions. Long ago he formed an ideal conception of omnipotence and omniscience, which he embodied in his gods, attributing to them whatever seemed beyond the reach of his desires – or was forbidden him. We may say, then, that these gods were cultural ideals. Man has now come close to reaching these ideals and almost become a god himself. Admittedly only in the way ideals are usually reached, according to the general judgement of humanity – not completely, in some respects not at all, in others only partly. Man has become, so to speak, a god with artificial limbs. He is quite impressive when he dons all his auxiliary organs, but they have not become part of him and still give him a good deal of trouble on occasion. However, he is entitled to console himself with the fact that this development will not have come to an end in AD 1930. Distant ages will bring new and probably unimaginable advances in this field of civilization and so enhance his god-like nature. But in the interest of our investigation let us also remember that modern man does not feel happy with his god-like nature.

We acknowledge, then, that a country has a high level of civilization if we find that in it everything that can assist man in his exploitation of the land and protect him against the forces of nature – everything, in short, that is of use to him – is attended to and properly ordered. In such countries, rivers that threaten to flood the land must have their courses regulated and their waters channelled to areas of drought. The soil must be carefully tilled and planted with crops that it is suited to support; the mineral wealth below ground must be diligently brought to the surface and used to make the necessary tools and implements. Means of transport must be frequent, fast and reliable. Dangerous wild beasts must be exterminated, and the breeding of domestic animals must flourish. But we have other demands to make on civilization and, remarkably, we hope to find them realized in the very same countries. As though we wished to repudiate our first demand, we also welcome it as a sign of civilization if people devote care to things that have no practical value whatever, that indeed appear useless – for instance, when the urban parks that are needed as playgrounds and reservoirs of fresh air also contain flowerbeds, or when the windows of the houses are adorned with pots of flowers. We soon realize that what we know to be useless, but expect civilization to value, is beauty; we demand that civilized man should revere beauty where he comes across it in nature and create it, if he can, through the work of his hands. Yet our claims on civilization are far from exhausted. We also demand evidence of cleanliness and order. We do not think highly of the civilization of an English country town in Shakespeare's day when we read that there was a large dunghill in front of the door of his father's house at Stratford. We are indignant and call it 'barbarous' – which is the opposite of 'civilized' – when we find the paths in the Vienna woods littered with discarded papers. Squalor of any kind seems to us incompatible with civilization, and we extend the demand for cleanliness to the human body too. We are amazed to read what a foul smell emanated from the person of the Roi Soleil, and we shake our heads when, on visiting Isola Bella, we are shown the tiny wash-basin that Napoleon used for his morning toilet. Indeed, we are not surprised if someone actually proposes the use of soap as a criterion of civilization. Much the same is true of order, which, like cleanliness, relates wholly to the work of man. But while we cannot expect cleanliness in nature, order is in fact copied from her; observation of the great astronomical regularities gave man not only the model for the introduction of order into his own life, but the first clues about how to do it. Order is a kind of compulsion to repeat, which, once a pattern is established, determines when, where and how something is to be done, so that there is no hesitation or vacillation in identical cases. The benefits of order are undeniable; it enables people to make the best use of space and time, while sparing their mental forces. One would be entitled to expect that it had established itself in human activities from the start and without any difficulty; and one may well be surprised that this is not so – that people show a natural tendency to be careless, irregular and unreliable in their work and must first be laboriously trained to imitate the celestial models.

Beauty, cleanliness and order plainly have a special place among the requirements of civilization. No one will maintain that they are as vitally important as control over the forces of nature and other factors that we shall become acquainted with later on, but neither will anyone wish to dismiss them as matters of minor importance. The fact that civilization is not concerned solely with utility is demonstrated by the example of beauty, which we insist on including among the interests of civilization. The usefulness of order is quite patent; as for cleanliness, we must bear in mind that it is also required by hygiene, and we may presume that people were not entirely unaware of this connection even before the age of scientific prophy-laxis. Yet utility does not wholly explain the striving for cleanliness: something else must be involved too.

No feature, however, seems to us to characterize civilization better than the appreciation and cultivation of the higher mental activities, of intellectual, scientific and artistic achievements, and the leading role accorded to ideas in human life. Foremost among these ideas are the systems of religion, on whose complex structure I have tried to throw some light elsewhere; next come philosophical speculations, and finally what may be called human ideals, the notions, formed by human beings, of the possible perfection of the individual person, the nation and humanity as a whole, together with the demands they set up on the basis of such notions. The fact that these inventions are not independent of one another, but closely interwoven, increases the difficulty not only of describing them, but of estab-lishing their psychological derivation. If we assume, quite generally, that the mainspring of all human activities is the striving for the two confluent goals of utility and the attainment of pleasure, we have to agree that this applies also to the manifestations of civilization that we have mentioned here, though it is easy to see only in the case of scientific and artistic activity. There can be no doubt, however, that the others also answer to powerful human needs, perhaps to needs that have developed only in a minority of people. Moreover, one must not allow oneself to be misled by value judgements regarding one or other of these religions, philosophical systems and ideals; one may think to find in them the highest achievement of the human spirit or deplore them as aberrations, but one has to acknowledge that their very existence, and especially their predominance, signifies a high level of civilization.

As the last and certainly not the least important characteristic of a civilization we have to consider how the mutual relations of human beings are regulated, the social relations that affect a person as a neighbour, employee or sexual object of another, as a member of a family or as a citizen of a state. Here it becomes particularly difficult to keep oneself free from certain ideal requirements and to grasp what pertains to civilization in general. Perhaps one may begin by declaring that the element of civilization is present as soon as the first attempt is made to regulate these social relations. If no such attempt were made, they would be subject to the arbitrary will of the individual; that is to say, whoever was physically stronger would dictate them in accordance with his interests and instinctual impulses. Nor would anything be changed if this strong individual came up against another who was even stronger. Communal life becomes possible only when a majority comes together that is stronger than any individual and presents a united front against every individual. The power of the community then pits itself, in the name of 'right', against the power of the individual, which is condemned as 'brute force'. The replacement of the power of the individual by that of the community is the decisive step towards civilization. Its essence lies in the fact that the members of the community restrict themselves in their scope for satisfaction; whereas the individual knew no such restriction. Hence, the next requirement of civilization is justice, that is the assurance that the legal order, once established, shall not be violated again in favour of an individual. This entails no judgement regarding the ethical value of such a system of law. The subsequent development of civilization seems to aim at a situation in which the law should no longer express the will of a small community – a caste, a social stratum or a tribe – that in its turn relates like a violent individual to other groups, which may be more comprehensive. The ultimate outcome should be a system of law to which all – or at least all those who qualify as members of the community – have contributed by partly forgoing the satisfaction of their drives, and which allows no one – again subject to the same qualification – to become a victim of brute force.

Individual liberty is not an asset of civilization. It was greatest before there was any civilization, though admittedly even then it was largely worthless, because the individual was hardly in a position to defend it. With the development of civilization it underwent restrictions, and justice requires that no one shall be spared these restrictions. Whatever makes itself felt in a human community as an urge for freedom may amount to a revolt against an existing injustice, thus favouring a further advance of civilization and remaining compatible with it. But it may spring from what remains of the original personality, still untamed by civilization, and so become a basis for hostility to civilization. The urge for freedom is thus directed against particular forms and claims of civilization, or against civilization as a whole. It does not seem as though any influence can induce human beings to change their nature and become like termites; they will probably always defend their claim to individual freedom against the will of the mass. Much of mankind's struggle is taken up with the task of finding a suitable, that is to say a happy accommodation, between the claims of the individual and the mass claims of civilization. One of the problems affecting the fate of mankind is whether such an accommodation can be achieved through a particular moulding of civilization or whether the conflict is irreconcilable.

By allowing common feeling to tell us what features of human life may count as civilized, we have gained a distinct impression or overall picture of civilization, though at first without learning anything that is not generally known. At the same time we have taken care not to concur with the prejudice that civilization is synonymous with a trend towards perfection, a path to perfection that is pre-ordained for mankind. Yet now we are faced with a view that perhaps leads somewhere else. The development of civilization appears to us as a peculiar process that humanity undergoes and in which some things strike us as familiar. We may characterize this process by citing the changes it brings about in well-known dispositions of the human drives, whose satisfaction is, after all, the economic task of our lives. Some of these drives are used up in such a way that in their place something appears that in an individual we describe as a character trait. The most curious example of this process is found in the anal eroticism of young human beings. Their original interest in the excretory function, in the organs and the products involved in it, is transformed as they grow older into a group of traits that we know as thrift, a sense of order and cleanliness, which, while valuable and welcome in themselves, may intensify and become predominant, thus producing what is called the anal character. How this happens we do not know, but there is no doubt that this view is correct. We have now found that order and cleanliness are essential requirements of civilization, though it is not altogether obvious that they are vitally necessary, any more than it is obvious that they are sources of pleasure. At this point we could not fail to be struck at first by the similarity between the process of civilization and the libidinal development of the individual. Other drives are induced to shift the conditions for their satisfaction, to direct them on to other paths; in most cases this coincides with *sublimation* (of the aims of the drives), with which we are familiar, but in some the two may still be kept apart. Sublimation of the drives is a particularly striking feature of cultural development, which makes it possible for the higher mental activities – scientific, artistic and ideological – to play such a signifi- cant role in civilized life. Yielding to a first impression, one is tempted to say that sublimation is a fate that civilization imposes on the drives. But one would do better to reflect on the matter a little longer. Thirdly – and this seems the most important point – it is impossible to overlook the extent to which civilization is built up on renunciation, how much it presupposes the non-satisfaction of powerful drives – by suppression, repression or some other means. Such 'cultural frustration' dominates the large sphere of interper- sonal relations; as we already know, it is the cause of the hostility that all civilizations have to contend with. It will also make serious demands on our scientific work; in this connection we have much to explain. It is not easy to understand how it is possible to deprive a drive of satisfaction. It cannot be done without risk; if there is no economic compensation, one can expect serious disturbances.

However, if we want to know what value can be claimed by our conception of the development of civilization as a particular process, comparable with the normal maturation of the individual, we clearly have to address another problem and ask ourselves to what influ-

ences the development of civilization owes its origin, how it emerged
and what has determined its course.

Notes

1. See *Die Zukunft einer Illusion* [*The Future of an Illusion*], 1927 [I]
(*Gesammelte Werke*, vol. XIV).
2. Psychoanalytic material, while incomplete and impossible to interpret
with any certainty, at least allows a surmise – a fantastic-sounding one –
about the origin of this great human achievement. It is as though primitive
man was in the habit, when confronted with fire, of using it to satisfy an
infantile desire by urinating on it and so putting it out. Extant legends leave
us in no doubt about the original phallic interpretation of the tongues of
flame stretching upwards. Extinguishing a fire by urinating on it – an activity
still resorted to by the latter-day giants Gulliver in Lilliput and Rabelais'
Gargantua – was therefore like a sexual act performed with a man, an
enjoyment of male potency in homosexual rivalry. Whoever first renounced
this pleasure and spared the fire was able to take it away with him and make
it serve his purposes. By damping down the fire of his own sexual excitement
he had subdued the natural force of fire. This great cultural conquest would
thus be the reward for forgoing the satisfaction of a drive. Moreover, it is as
though the man had charged the woman with guarding the fire, now held
prisoner on the domestic hearth, because her anatomy made it impossible
for her to yield to such a temptation. It is remarkable too how regularly
analytic findings testify to the link between ambition, fire and urinal
eroticism.

IV

The task seems immense, and one may freely admit to being daunted by it. Here are the few conjectures I have been able to arrive at.

When primitive man had discovered that he had it in his own hands – quite literally – to improve his earthly lot by working, it could no longer be a matter of indifference to him whether someone else was working with him or against him. This other person now acquired for him the value of a fellow-worker, and it was useful to him if they both lived together. Even earlier, in his ape-like prehistory, man had taken to forming families, and members of the family were probably his first helpers. Presumably the founding of the family was linked with the fact that the need for genital satisfaction no longer made its appearance like a guest who turns up suddenly one day, then leaves and is not heard of again for a long time, but moved in as a permanent lodger. Hence, the male acquired a motive for keeping the female or – to put it more generally – his sexual objects around him, while the females, not wanting to be separated from their helpless young, had for their sake to remain with the stronger male.[1] In this primitive family we note the absence of one essential feature of civilization: the arbitrary power of the father, the head of the family, was absolute. In *Totem and Taboo* I tried to trace the route that led from this family to the next stage of communal living, which took the form of bands of brothers. On overpowering their father, the sons found that the group could be stronger than the individual. Totemic culture rests upon the restrictions they had to impose on one another in order to sustain this new state of affairs. Taboo observances constituted the first system of 'law'. There were thus two reasons why human beings should live together: one was the compulsion to work, which was created by external hardship; the other was the power of love, which made the man loath to dispense with his sexual object, the woman, and the woman loath to surrender her child, which had once been part of her. Eros and Ananke (Love and Necessity) thus become the progenitors of human civilization too. The first consequence of civilization was that even fairly large numbers of people could now stay together in a community. And because these two powerful forces worked in concert, future developments could be expected to proceed smoothly towards better and better control of the external world and the extension of the community to take in more and more people. Moreover, it is not easy to see how this civilization could be anything but a source of happiness to its participants.

Before we go on to consider where a disturbance might arise, let us allow ourselves to be deflected by the recognition of love as a foundation for civilization; in this way we can fill a gap in our earlier discussion. We said that, since sexual (genital) love had afforded man the most potent experiences of satisfaction and had actually supplied him with the model for all happiness, this should have told him that he would do well to go on seeking his happiness in the sphere of sexual relations and place genital eroticism at the centre of his life. We went on to say that by doing this one made oneself dangerously dependent on part of the external world, the chosen love-object, that one was exposed to extreme suffering if one was spurned by it or lost it through infidelity or death. For this reason sages in every age have emphatically advised against this way of conducting one's life, but it has not yet lost its attraction for much of humankind.

A small minority of people are enabled by their constitution, in spite of everything, to find happiness through love, though this necessitates great psychical modifications of its function. These people make themselves independent of the concurrence of the object of their love by shifting the main emphasis from being loved to their own loving; they protect themselves against the loss of the love object by directing their love not to individuals, but to everyone in equal measure, and they avoid the uncertainties and disappointments of genital love by deviating from its sexual aim and transforming the drive into an *aim-inhibited* impulse. What they thereby create in themselves – a state of balanced, unwavering, affectionate feeling – no longer bears much outward resemblance to the turbulent genital love-life from which it none the less derives. Perhaps St Francis of Assisi went furthest in exploiting love in this way to gain a feeling of inner happiness; moreover, what we recognize as one of the techniques for fulfilling the pleasure principle has frequently been associated with religion, with which it may be connected in those remote regions where the differentiation of the ego from the objects or the objects from one another is neglected. One ethical view, whose deeper motivation will presently become obvious, sees this readiness to love mankind and the world in general as the highest attitude to which human beings can attain. Even at this early stage we will not withhold our two main reservations: first, an undiscriminating love seems to us to forfeit some of its intrinsic value by doing its object an injustice, and, secondly, not all human beings are worthy of love.

The love that founded the family remains effective in civilization, both in its original form, in which direct sexual satisfaction is not renounced, and in its modified form as aim-inhibited affection. In both it continues to perform the function of binding together fairly large numbers of people, and it does so more intensively than would be possible on the basis of a common interest in work. The careless way in which the language uses the word 'love' can be justified historically. The word denotes not only the relation between a man and a woman, whose genital needs have led them to found a family, but also the positive feelings that exist within the family between parents and children, and between siblings, though we are bound to describe the latter relation as aim-inhibited love or affection. This aim-inhibited love was in fact once a fully sensual love, and it still is in the individual's unconscious. Both fully sensual and aim-inhibited love extend outside the family and create new bonds with people who were previously strangers. Genital love leads to the formation of new families, and aim-inhibited love to 'friendships', which become important for civilization because they avoid some of the restrictions of genital love, such as its exclusivity. But as it develops, the relation of love to civilization ceases to be unequivocal. On the one hand, love comes into conflict with the interests of civilization; on the other, civilization threatens love with substantial restrictions.

This rift seems unavoidable, but its cause is not at once discernible. It first manifests itself as a conflict between the family and the wider community to which the individual belongs. We have already noted that one of civilization's chief endeavours is to bring people together in large units. However, the family will not give up the individual. The closer the solidarity of the family, the more often its members tend to cut themselves off from other people and the harder it is for them to enter into the wider circle of life. The phylogenetically older mode of living together – the only one that exists in childhood – resists being superseded by the civilized one that was acquired later. Detaching oneself from the family is a task that faces every young person, and society often supports him in performing it with puberty and initiation rites. One has the impression that such difficulties attach to any psychical development, indeed to any organic development.

Moreover, women soon come into conflict with the cultural trend and exercise a retarding, restraining influence on it, even though it was they who first laid the foundations of civilization with the claims of their love. Women stand for the interests of the family and sexual life, whereas the work of civilization has become more and more the business of the menfolk, setting them increasingly difficult tasks and obliging them to sublimate their drives – a task for which women have little aptitude. No person has unlimited quantities of psychical energy at his disposal, and so he has to accomplish his tasks through an expedient distribution of the libido. Whatever energy he expends on cultural aims is largely denied to the opposite sex: his constant association with men and his dependency on this association even estrange him from his duties as a husband and father. The woman therefore sees herself forced into the background by the claims of civilization and adopts a hostile attitude to it.

Civilization's tendency to restrict sexual life is no less clear than its other tendency – to extend the cultural circle. The first phase of civilization, the totemic phase, already involves the prohibition of incest in the choice of one's sexual object; this is perhaps the most drastic mutilation that man's erotic life has experienced throughout the ages. Taboo, law and custom create further restrictions, affecting both men and women. Not all civilizations go to the same lengths; and the economic structure of society influences the degree of sexual freedom that remains. We already know that in this respect civilization follows the dictates of economic necessity, because it deprives sexuality of much of the mental energy that it consumes. Civilization thus behaves towards sexuality like a tribe or a section of the population that has subjected another and started exploiting it. Fear that the victims may rebel necessitates strict precautionary measures. A high point in such a development can be seen in our western European civilization. It is psychologically quite justified to begin by prohibiting expressions of infantile sexuality, for there is no prospect of curbing the sexual appetites of adults unless preparatory measures have been taken in childhood. Yet civilized society cannot in any way be justified in going further and actually denying these phenomena, which are easily demonstrable, indeed striking. The sexually mature individual finds that his choice of object is restricted to the opposite sex, and that most extra-genital gratifications are forbidden as perversions. The demand for a uniform sexual life for all, which is proclaimed in all these prohibitions, disregards all the disparities, innate and acquired, in the sexual constitution of human beings, thereby depriving fairly large numbers of sexual enjoyment and becoming a source of grave injustice. The result of such restrictions might be that in normal persons – those who are not constitutionally inhibited – all sexual interest would flow, with no loss, into the channels still left open to it. But what is not outlawed – heterosexual genital love – is still limited by legitimacy and monogamy. Present-day civilization makes it clear that it will permit sexual relations only on the basis of a unique and indissoluble bond between a man and a woman, that it disapproves of sexuality as a source of pleasure in its own right and will tolerate it only as the device – for which a substitute has still to be found – for the increase of mankind.

This is of course an extreme view, and it is known to have proved impracticable, even for quite short periods. Only the weaklings have acquiesced in such a gross invasion of their sexual freedom; stronger spirits have insisted on a compensatory condition, which can be mentioned later. Civilized society has found itself obliged to turn a blind eye to many transgressions that by its own lights it should have punished. Yet one must not err in the opposite direction and assume that such a cultural attitude is altogether innocuous because it does not do all it sets out to do. After all, the sexual life of civilized man has been seriously damaged; at times one has the impression that as a function it is subject to a process of involution, such as our teeth and our hair seem to be undergoing as organs. One is probably entitled to suppose that its importance as a source of happiness – and therefore as a means to fulfil our purpose in life – has perceptibly diminished.[2] Now and then one seems to realize that this is not just the pressure of civilization, but that something inherent in the function itself denies us total satisfaction and forces us on to other paths. This may be wrong – it is hard to decide.[3]

Notes

1. The organic periodicity of the sexual process had been retained, but its influence on psychical sexual excitation was reversed. This change was most probably connected with the decline of the olfactory stimuli by which the menstrual process affected the male psyche. Their role was taken over by visual excitations, which differed from the intermittent olfactory stimuli in that they could remain permanently effective. The taboo on menstruation stems from this 'organic repression', as a defence against a phase of development that has been surmounted; all other motivations are probably of a secondary nature. (Cf. C. D. Daly, 'Hindumythologie und Kastrationskomplex', *Imago* XIII, 1927.) This process is replicated at a different level when the gods of a past cultural period become the demons of the next. However, the decline of the olfactory stimuli itself seems to have resulted from man's decision to adopt an upright gait, which meant that the genitals, previously hidden, became visible and in need of protection, thus giving rise to a sense of shame. The beginning of the fateful process of civilization, then, would

have been marked by man's adopting of an erect posture. From then on the chain of events proceeded, by way of the devaluation of the olfactory stimuli and the isolation of the menstrual period, to the preponderance of the visual stimuli and the visibility of the genitals, then to the continuity of sexual excitation and the founding of the family, and so to the threshold of human civilization. This is merely theoretical speculation, but it is sufficiently important to deserve to be precisely tested against the conditions of life obtaining among those animals that are closely related to man.

There is an unmistakable social factor in the cultural striving for cleanliness too, which was later justified on grounds of hygiene, but manifested itself before this connection was appreciated. The urge for cleanliness arises from the wish to get rid of excrement, which has become repugnant to the senses. In the nursery, as we know, things are different. Excrement does not arouse any disgust in the child; it seems valuable to him as a part of his body that has become detached. Upbringing here insists on accelerating the future course of development, which will make excrement worthless, disgusting, revolting and abominable. Such a reversal of values would be scarcely possible if this material excreted by the body were not condemned by its strong smell to share the fate that overtook the olfactory stimuli after man adopted an erect posture. Hence, anal eroticism first yields to the 'organic repression' that paved the way for civilization. Evidence of the social factor, leading to the further transformation of anal eroticism, is found in the fact that, all evolutionary progress notwithstanding, human beings hardly find the smell of their own excrement offensive – only that of others. A person who lacks cleanliness – who does not hide his excrement – thereby offends others and shows them no consideration, and this is reflected in our strongest and commonest terms of abuse. It would also be incomprehensible that man should use the name of his most faithful friend in the animal world as a term of abuse, were it not for the fact that the dog incurs his contempt through two of its characteristics: as an animal that relies on smell it does not shun excrement, and it is not ashamed of its sexual functions.

2. Among the works of the sensitive and now widely esteemed English writer John Galsworthy is a short story called 'The Apple-Tree', of which I formed a high opinion years ago. It shows very cogently how the life of civilized people today no longer has room for the simple, natural love of two human beings.

3. The following observations are offered in support of the supposition made above. Man too is an animal with an unequivocally bisexual disposition. The individual represents a fusion of two symmetrical halves; one of these, in the opinion of some investigators, is purely male, the other female. It is

equally possible that each half was originally hermaphrodite. Sexuality is a biological fact that is immensely important in our psychical life, but it is hard to comprehend psychologically. We are in the habit of saying that every human being exhibits both male and female impulses, needs and properties, but while anatomy can distinguish between male and female, psychology cannot. In the latter discipline the contrast between 'male' and 'female' pales into one between 'active' and 'passive'. We do not hesitate to equate 'active' with 'male' and 'passive' with 'female', but these equations are by no means universally confirmed by the study of animals. The theory of bisexuality is still shrouded in obscurity, and the fact that it has not been connected with that of the drives is bound to strike us as a serious flaw in psychoanalysis. Be that as it may, if we take it to be a fact that every individual seeks to satisfy both male and female desires in his or her sexual life, we are prepared for the possibility that these are not fulfilled by the same object and that they interfere with one another unless they can be kept apart and each impulse can be guided into the proper channel. A further difficulty arises because erotic relations are so often associated with a degree of direct aggression, quite apart from the sadistic component that properly belongs to them. Faced with such complications, the love-object will not always be as understanding and tolerant as the farmer's wife who complained that her husband no longer loved her because he had not beaten her for a week.

The surmise that goes deepest, however, is one that arises from my remarks in the footnote [section IV, note 1], to the effect that, with man's adoption of an upright posture and the devaluation of his sense of smell, the whole of his sexuality – not just his anal eroticism – was in danger of becoming subject to organic repression, so that the sexual function has since been accompanied by an unaccountable repugnance, which prevents total gratification and deflects it from the sexual aim towards sublimations and displacements of the libido. I know that some time ago Bleuler ('Der Sexualwiderstand', *Jahrbuch für psychoanalytische und psychopathologische Forschungen* V [1913]) pointed to the existence of an original aversion to sexual life. All neurotics, and many others, object to the fact that *inter urinas et faeces nascimur* ('we are born between urine and faeces'). The genitals give off strong smells that are intolerable to many and spoil their enjoyment of sexual intercourse. Hence, the ultimate root of the sexual repression that accompanies cultural progress would seem to be the organic defence of the new way of life, ushered in by man's adoption of an upright gait, against his earlier animal existence. This result of scientific research coincides in a curious way with a banal prejudice that is often voiced.

However, these are at present merely unconfirmed possibilities that lack any scientific corroboration. And let us not forget that, in spite of the undoubted devaluation of olfactory stimuli, there are certain peoples, even in Europe, for whom the pungent genital odours we find offensive are valuable sexual stimuli, which they would be loath to forgo. (See the folkloric findings of Iwan Bloch's questionnaire on 'the sense of smell in sexual life', published in various issues of the *Anthropophyteia* of Friedrich S. Krauss.)

V

Psychoanalytic work has taught us that it is precisely these frustrations of sexual life that those whom we call neurotics cannot endure. Neurotics create substitutive satisfactions for themselves in their symptoms, but these either create suffering in themselves or become sources of suffering by causing the subjects difficulties in their relations with their surroundings and society. The latter fact is easy to understand, but the former poses a fresh puzzle. However, civilization demands other sacrifices apart from that of sexual satisfaction.

We have viewed the difficulty of cultural development as a general difficulty of development by tracing it back to the inertia of the libido, to the latter's unwillingness to give up an old position for a new one. We are saying much the same thing when we derive the opposition between civilization and sexuality from the fact that sexual love is a relationship between two people, in which a third party can only be superfluous or troublesome, whereas civilization rests on relations between quite large numbers of people. When a love relationship is at its height, the lovers no longer have any interest in the world around them; they are self-sufficient as a pair, and in order to be happy they do not even need the child they have in common. In no other case does Eros so clearly reveal what is at the core of his being, the aim of making one out of more than one; however, having achieved this proverbial goal by making two people fall in love, he refuses to go any further.

Up to now we can well imagine a cultural community consisting of such double individuals, libidinally sated in themselves, but linked by the bonds of shared work and interests. If this were so it would not be necessary for civilization to rob sexuality of any of its energy.

But this desirable state of affairs does not exist, and never has. Reality shows us that civilization is not satisfied with the bonds that have so far been conceded to it; it seeks also to bind the members of the community libidinally to one another, employing every available means to this end, favouring any path that leads to strong identifications among them, and summoning up the largest possible measure of aim-inhibited libido in order to reinforce the communal bonds with ties of friendship. For the fulfilment of these objectives the restriction of sexual life becomes inevitable. Yet we lack any understanding of the necessity that forces civilization along this path and can account for its opposition to sexuality. There must be a disturbing factor that we have not yet discovered.

One of what have been called the ideal demands of civilized society may put us on the right track. It runs: 'Thou shalt love thy neighbour as thyself.' It is famous the world over, and certainly older than Christianity, which puts it forward as its proudest claim, but assuredly not very old, for in historical times it still struck people as strange. We will approach it naively, as if we were hearing it for the first time. We shall then be unable to suppress a sense of surprise and bewilderment. Why should we behave in this way? What good will it do us? But above all, how shall we manage to act like this? How will it be possible? My love is something I value and must not throw away irresponsibly. It imposes duties on me, and in performing these duties I must be prepared to make sacrifices. If I love another person, he must in some way deserve it. (I will disregard whatever use he may be to me, and whatever importance he may have for me as a sexual object: these two kinds of relationship have no relevance to the injunction to love my neighbour.) He deserves it if, in certain important respects, he so much resembles me that in him I can love myself. He deserves it if he is so much more perfect than myself that I can love in him an ideal image of myself. I must love him if he is my friend's son, for the pain my friend would feel if any harm befell him would be my pain too; I should have to share it. But if he is a stranger to me and cannot attract me by any merit of his own or by any importance he has acquired in my emotional life, it becomes hard for me to love him. Indeed, it would be wrong of me to do so,

46

for my love is prized by my family and friends as a sign of my preference for them; to put a stranger on a par with them would be to do them an injustice. Yet if I am to love him, with this universal love – just because he is a creature of this earth, like an insect, an earthworm or a grass-snake – then I fear that only a modicum of love will fall to his share, and certainly not as much as the judgement of my reason entitles me to reserve for myself. What is the point of such a portentous precept if its fulfilment cannot commend itself as reasonable?

On closer inspection I find still more difficulties. This stranger is not only altogether unlovable: I must honestly confess that he has a greater claim to my enmity, even to my hatred. He appears to have not the least love for me and shows me not the slightest consideration. If it is to his advantage, he has no hesitation in harming me, nor does he ask himself whether the magnitude of his advantage is commensurate with the harm he does me. Indeed, it need not bring him any advantage at all: if he can merely satisfy some desire by acting in this way, he will think nothing of mocking, insulting or slandering me, or using me as a foil to show off his power. The more secure he feels and the more helpless I am, the surer I can be of his behaving towards me like this. If he acts differently towards me, a stranger, and treats me with consideration and forbearance, I am in any case ready to repay him in like coin, without any injunction to do so. Indeed, if this grandiose commandment were to read: 'Love thy neighbour as thy neighbour loves thee', I should have no quarrel with it. There is another commandment that I find even more unintelligible and that causes me to rebel even more fiercely. It runs: 'Love thine enemies.' But on reflection I see that I am wrong to reject it as a still greater presumption. Essentially it is no different.[1]

But now I seem to hear a dignified voice admonishing me: 'It is precisely because your neighbour is not lovable, but on the contrary your enemy, that you must love him as yourself.' I then understand this to be another instance of *Credo quia absurdum* ('I believe it because it is absurd').

Now, it is quite likely that my neighbour, if enjoined to love me as himself, will react exactly as I do and reject me for the very same reasons. I hope he will not have the same objective justification, but he will be of the same mind. However, there are differences in human behaviour that ethics classify as 'good' and 'evil', disregarding the fact that such differences are conditioned. While these undeniable differences remain, the fulfilment of these high ethical demands is detrimental to the purposes of civilization in that it proposes direct rewards for wrongful conduct. In this connection one cannot help recalling an incident that occurred in the French Chamber when capital punishment was being debated. One speaker pleaded passionately for its abolition and received tumultuous applause, until a voice called out from the body of the hall: 'Que messieurs les assassins commencent!' ['Let the murderers make the first move!']

The reality behind all this, which many would deny, is that human beings are not gentle creatures in need of love, at most able to defend themselves if attacked; on the contrary, they can count a powerful share of aggression among their instinctual endowments. Hence, their neighbour is not only a potential helper or sexual object, but also someone who tempts them to take out their aggression on him, to exploit his labour without recompense, to use him sexually without his consent, to take possession of his goods, to humiliate him and cause him pain, to torture and kill him. *Homo homini lupus* [Man is a wolf to man]. Who, after all that he has learnt from life and history, would be so bold as to dispute this proposition? As a rule, this cruel aggression waits for some provocation or puts itself at the service of a different aim, which could be attained by milder means. If the circumstances favour it, if the psychical counter-forces that would otherwise inhibit it have ceased to operate, it manifests itself spontaneously and reveals man as a savage beast that has no thought of sparing its own kind. Whoever calls to mind the horrors of the migrations of the peoples, the incursions of the Huns, or of the people known as the Mongols under Genghiz Khan and Tamerlane, the conquest of Jerusalem by the pious Crusaders, or indeed the horrors of the Great War, will be obliged to acknowledge this as a fact.

It is the existence of this tendency to aggression, which we detect in ourselves and rightly presume in others, that vitiates our relations with our neighbour and obliges civilization to go to such lengths. Given this fundamental hostility of human beings to one another, civilized society is constantly threatened with disintegration. A common interest in work would not hold it together: passions that derive from the drives are stronger than reasonable interests. Civilization has to make every effort to limit man's aggressive drives and hold down their manifestations through the formation of psychical reactions. This leads to the use of methods that are meant to encourage people to identify themselves with others and enter into aim-inhibited erotic relationships, to the restriction of sexual life, and also to the ideal commandment to love one's neighbour as oneself, which is actually justified by the fact that nothing else runs so much counter to basic human nature. For all the effort invested in it, this cultural endeavour has so far not achieved very much. It hopes to prevent the crudest excesses of brutal violence by assuming the right to use violence against criminals, but the law cannot deal with the subtler manifestations of human aggression. There comes a point at which each of us abandons, as illusions, the expectations he pinned to his fellow men when he was young and can appreciate how difficult and painful his life is made by their ill will. At the same time it would be unjust to reproach civilization with wanting to exclude contention and competition from human activity. These are certainly indispensable, but opposition is not necessarily enmity: it is merely misused as an occasion for the latter.

The communists think they have found the way to redeem mankind from evil. Man is unequivocally good and well disposed to his neighbour, but his nature has been corrupted by the institution of private property. Ownership of property gives the individual the power, and so the temptation, to mistreat his neighbour; whoever is excluded from ownership is bound to be hostile to the oppressor and rebel against him. When private property is abolished, when goods are held in common and enjoyed by all, ill will and enmity among human beings will cease. Because all needs will be satisfied, no one will have any reason to see another person as his enemy; everyone will be glad to undertake whatever work is necessary. I am not concerned with economic criticisms of the communist system; I have no way of knowing whether the abolition of private property is expedient and beneficial.[2] But I can recognize the psychological presumption behind it as a baseless illusion. With the abolition of private property the human love of aggression is robbed of one of its tools, a strong one no doubt, but certainly not the strongest. No change has been made in the disparities of power and influence that aggression exploits in pursuit of its ends, or in its nature. Aggression was not created by property; it prevailed with almost no restriction in primitive times, when property was very scanty. It already manifests itself in the nursery, where property has hardly given up its original anal form. It forms the basis of all affectionate and loving relations among human beings, with perhaps the one exception of the relation between the mother and her male child. Even if we do away with the personal right to own material goods, the prerogative that resides in sexual relations still remains, and this is bound to become the source of the greatest animosity and the fiercest enmity among human beings who are equal in all other respects. If we remove this inequality too and allow total sexual freedom – thus doing away with the family, the germ-cell of civilization – it will admittedly be impossible to foresee on what new paths the development of civilization may strike out. But of one thing we can be certain: this indestructible feature of human nature will follow it wherever it leads.

It is clearly not easy for people to forgo the satisfaction of their tendency to aggression. To do so makes them feel uneasy. One should not belittle the advantage that is enjoyed by a fairly small cultural circle, which is that it allows the aggressive drive an outlet in the form of hostility to outsiders. It is always possible to bind quite large numbers of people together in love, provided that others are left out as targets for aggression. I once discussed this phenomenon, the fact that it is precisely those communities that occupy contiguous territories and are otherwise closely related to each other – like the Spaniards and the Portuguese, the North Germans and the South Germans, the English and the Scots, etc. – that indulge in feuding and mutual mockery. I called this phenomenon 'the narcissism of small differences' – not that the name does much to explain it. It can be seen as a convenient and relatively innocuous way of satisfying the tendency to aggression and facilitating solidarity within the community. The Jews of the diaspora have made valuable contributions to the cultures of the countries in which they have settled, but unfortunately all the massacres of Jews that took place in the Middle Ages failed to make the age safer and more peaceful for the Christians. After St Paul had made universal brotherly love the foundation of his Christian community, the extreme intolerance of Christianity towards those left outside it was an inevitable consequence. To the Romans, whose state was not founded on love, religious intolerance had been quite foreign, though religion was a state concern and the state was steeped in religion. Nor was it quite fortuitous and incomprehensible that the Germanic dream of world-dominion should invoke anti-semitism as its complement. And it is understandable that the attempt to establish a new, communist culture in Russia should find psychological support in the persecution of the bourgeois. One only wonders, with some anxiety, what the Soviets will turn to when they have exterminated their bourgeoisie.

If civilization imposes such great sacrifices not only on man's sexuality, but also on his aggressivity, we are in a better position to understand why it is so hard for him to feel happy in it. Primitive man was actually better off, because his drives were not restricted. Yet this was counterbalanced by the fact that he had little certainty of enjoying this good fortune for long. Civilized man has traded in a portion of his chances of happiness for a certain measure of security. But let us not forget that in the primeval family only its head could give full rein to his drives; its other members lived in slavish suppression. In that primordial era of civilization there was therefore an extreme contrast between a minority who enjoyed its benefits and the majority to whom they were denied. As for today's primitive peoples, more careful study has shown that we have no reason whatever to envy them their instinctual life by reason of the freedom attaching to it; it is subject to restrictions of a different kind, which are perhaps even more severe than those imposed on modern civilized man.

When we rightly reproach the present state of our civilization with its inadequate response to our demand for a form of life that will make us happy, and with allowing so much suffering, which could probably be avoided – and when we strive, with unsparing criticism, to expose the roots of this inadequacy – we are exercising a legitimate right and certainly not revealing ourselves as enemies of civilization. We may hope gradually to carry out such modifications in our civilization as will better satisfy our needs and escape this criticism. But perhaps we shall also become familiar with the idea that there are some difficulties that are inherent in the nature of civilization and will defy any attempt at reform. In addition to the tasks involved in restricting the drives – for which we are prepared – we are faced with the danger of a condition that we may call 'the psychological misery of the mass'. This danger is most threatening where social bonding is produced mainly by the participants' identification with one another, while individuals of leadership calibre do not acquire the importance that should be accorded to them in the formation of the mass.[3] The present state of American civilization would provide a good opportunity to study the cultural damage that is to be feared. But I shall avoid the temptation to engage in a critique of American civilization; I do not wish to give the impression of wanting to employ American methods myself.

Notes

1. A great writer can allow himself, at least in jest, to express psychological truths that incur severe disapproval. Heine, for instance, confesses: 'I have the most peaceable disposition. My wishes are: a modest cottage with a thatched roof, but a good bed, good food, milk and butter, very fresh, flowers in front of the window, a few beautiful trees in front of the door; and if the good Lord wants to make me completely happy, he will grant me the pleasure of seeing six or seven of my enemies hanged from these trees. My heart will be moved, and before they die I will forgive them all the wrongs they did me in their lifetime. Yes, one must forgive one's enemies, but not before they are hanged' (Heinrich Heine, *Gedanken und Einfälle*).
2. Anyone who has tasted the misery of poverty in his youth and experienced

the indifference and arrogance of propertied people, should be safe from the suspicion that he has no sympathy with current efforts to combat inequalities of wealth and all that flows from them. Of course, if this struggle seeks to appeal to the abstract demand, made in the name of justice, for equality among all men, the objection is all too obvious: nature, by her highly unequal endowment of individuals with physical attributes and mental abilities, has introduced injustices that cannot be remedied.

3. See *Massenpsychologie und Ich-Analyse* [*Group Psychology and the Analysis of the Ego*], 1921 [VII] (*Gesammelte Werke*, vol. XIII).

VI

With none of my writings have I had such a strong feeling as I have now that what I am describing is common knowledge, that I am using pen and paper, and shall soon be using the services of the compositor and the printer, to say things that are in fact self-evident. For this reason I shall be glad to take the matter up if it appears that the recognition of a special, independent aggressive drive entails a modification of psychoanalytic theory regarding the drives.

It will be seen that this is not so, that it is merely a matter of focusing more sharply on a change of direction that took place long ago, and of following up its consequences. Of all the elements of analytic theory that have taken so long to develop, the doctrine of the drives is the one that has edged its way forward most laboriously. And yet it was so indispensable to the whole that something had to be put in its place. After I had at first been totally at a loss, my first clue came from a proposition by the poet-philosopher Schiller, to the effect that the mechanism of the world was held together by 'hunger and love'. Hunger could be taken to represent those drives that seek to preserve the individual creature, whereas love strives after objects, and its chief function, favoured in every way by nature, is to preserve the species. Thus at first ego-drives and object-drives confronted one another. To denote the energy of the latter – and them alone – I introduced the term 'libido'; there was thus a contrast between the ego-drives and the libidinal drives of love, in the widest sense of the word, which were directed towards an object. One of these latter, the sadistic drive, admittedly stood out from the rest because its aim was so utterly devoid of love. Moreover, in some respects it was obviously attached to the ego-drives; it could not conceal its close affinity to the drives that aim at domination and have no libidinal purpose. However, it proved possible to get over this discrepancy: after all, sadism was clearly part of sexual life, in which cruelty could replace tenderness. Neurosis appeared to be the result of a struggle between the interest of self-preservation and the demands of the libido, a struggle in which the ego had triumphed, but at the price of grave suffering and sacrifice.

Every analyst will admit that even today this does not sound like a long-discarded error. Yet a modification became indispensable when our research proceeded from what was repressed to the agent of repression, from the object-drives to the ego. The decisive step here was the introduction of the concept of narcissism – that is to say the recognition that the ego itself is occupied by libido, that it is in fact the libido's original home and remains to some extent its headquarters. This narcissistic libido turns towards objects, thus becoming object-libido, and can change back again into narcissistic libido. The concept of narcissism made it possible to understand and analyse traumatic neurosis, together with many other conditions that are closely related to the psychoses, as well as the psychoses themselves. There was no need to abandon the interpretation of transference neuroses as attempts by the ego to fend off sexuality, but the concept of libido was endangered. Since the ego-drives too were libidinal, it seemed for a time inevitable that the libido should be allowed to merge with the energy of the drives generally, as C. G. Jung had earlier advocated. Yet there remained something like a certainty, as yet unexplained, that the drives could not all be of the same kind. My next step was taken in *Beyond the Pleasure Principle* (1920), when I was first struck by the compulsion to repeat and the conservative nature of the drives. Starting from speculations about the beginning of life and from biological parallels, I reached the conclusion that, in addition to the drive to preserve the living substance and bring it together in ever larger units,[1] there must be another, opposed to it, which sought to break down these units and restore them to their primordial inorganic state. Beside Eros, then, there was a death drive, and the interaction and counteraction of these two could explain the phenomena of life. Now, it was not easy to demonstrate the activity of this supposed death drive. The manifestations of Eros were plain enough to see and hear; one might presume that the death drive operated silently inside the living being, working towards its dissolution, but this of course did not amount to a proof. A more fruitful idea was that a portion of the drive was directed against the external world and then appeared as a drive that aimed at aggression and destruction. In this way the drive was itself pressed into the service of Eros, inasmuch as the organism destroyed other things, both animate and inanimate, instead of itself. Conversely, any restriction of this outward-directed aggression would be bound to increase the degree of self-destruction, which in any case continued. At the same time one could surmise, on the basis of this example, that the two kinds of drive seldom – perhaps never – appeared in isolation, but alloyed with one another in different and highly varying proportions and so became unrecognizable to our judgement. In sadism, which has long been recognized as a partial drive of sexuality, one would be faced with a particularly strong alloy of the striving for love and the drive for destruction, just as its counterpart, masochism, would be a combination of inward-directed destruction and sexuality, through which the otherwise imperceptible striving became conspicuous and palpable.

The assumption of a death drive or a drive for destruction has met with resistance even in analytic circles; I am aware that there is a widespread tendency to ascribe anything that is thought to be dangerous or hostile about love to an original bipolarity in its own nature. The views I have developed here were at first put forward only tentatively, but in the course of time they have taken such a hold on me that I can no longer think in any other way. In my view they are theoretically far more serviceable than any others one might entertain; they produce what we strive for in scientific work – a simple answer that neither neglects nor does violence to the facts. I recognize that we have always seen sadism and masochism as manifestations of the destructive drive, directed outwards or inwards and strongly alloyed with eroticism, but I can no longer understand how we could have ignored the ubiquity of non-erotic aggression and destruction and failed to accord it its due place in the interpretation of life. (The inward-directed craving for destruction mostly eludes our perception, of course, unless it is tinged with eroticism.) I can remember how I myself resisted the idea of a destructive drive when it first appeared in psychoanalytic literature, and how long it took me to become receptive to it. That others rejected it too, and still do, I find less surprising. 'For the little children do not like it' when there is talk of man's inborn tendency to 'wickedness', to aggression and destruction, and therefore to cruelty. For God created them in his own perfect image; one does not wish to be reminded of how hard it is to reconcile the existence of evil, which cannot be denied – despite the protestations of Christian Science – with His infinite power and goodness. The Devil would be the best excuse for God; he would take on the same exculpatory role in this context as the Jew in the world of the Aryan ideal. But even so, one can still demand that God be held responsible for the existence of the Devil and the evil he embodies. In view of these difficulties, it is advisable for each of us, at an appropriate point, to make a profound obeisance to man's deeply moral nature; this will help to make us generally popular, and much will be forgiven us.[2]

The name 'libido' can once more be applied to manifestations of the power of Eros, in order to distinguish them from the energy of the death drive.[3] It has to be admitted that the latter is much harder to grasp and can to some extent be discerned only as a residue left behind by Eros, and that it escapes our notice unless it is revealed through being alloyed with Eros. It is in sadism, where it perverts the erotic aim for its own purposes while fully satisfying the sexual striving, that we have the clearest insight into its nature and its relation to Eros. Yet even where it appears without any sexual purpose, in the blindest destructive fury, there is no mistaking the fact that its satisfaction is linked with an extraordinarily high degree of narcissistic enjoyment, in that this satisfaction shows the ego how its old wish for omnipotence can be fulfilled. Moderated and tamed – aim-inhibited, as it were – the destructive drive, when directed towards objects, must provide the ego with the satisfaction of its vital needs and with control over nature. As its existence is posited essentially on theoretical grounds, one must also admit that it is not wholly proof against theoretical objections. But this is how things appear to us now, in the present state of our knowledge; future research and reflection will undoubtedly bring the decisive clarification.

For the rest, I take the view that the tendency to aggression is an original, autonomous disposition in man, and I return to my earlier contention that it represents the greatest obstacle to civilization. At one point in this investigation we were faced with the realization that civilization was a special process undergone by humanity, and we are still under the spell of this idea. We will now add that it is a process in the service of Eros, whose purpose is to gather together individuals, then families and finally tribes, peoples and nations in one great unit – humanity. Why this has to happen we do not know: it is simply the work of Eros. These multitudes of human beings are to be libidinally bound to one another; necessity alone, the advantages of shared work, will not hold them together. However, this programme of civilization is opposed by man's natural aggressive drive, the hostility of each against all and all against each. This aggressive drive is the descendant and principal representative of the death drive, which we have found beside Eros and which rules the world jointly with him. And now, I think, the meaning of the development of civilization is no longer obscure to us. This development must show us the struggle between Eros and death, between the life drive and the drive for destruction, as it is played out in the human race. This struggle is the essential content of all life; hence, the development of civilization may be described simply as humanity's struggle for existence.[4] And this battle of the giants is what our nurse-maids seek to mitigate with their lullaby about heaven.

similar to CATABOLISM

Notes

1. The contrast that emerges here between the restless expansive tendency of Eros and the generally conservative nature of the drives is striking and could become the starting point for the study of further problems.

2. Especially convincing is the equation of the principle of evil with the destructive drive in the person of Goethe's Mephistopheles:

> *Denn alles, was entsteht,*
> *Ist wert, dass es zugrunde geht.*
> . . .
>
> *So ist denn alles, was Ihr Sünde,*
> *Zerstörung, kurz das Böse nennt,*
> *Mein eigentliches Element.*

[For everything that comes into being is worthy of destruction . . . So, then, everything you call sin, destruction – in short, evil – is my true element.]

As his adversary, the devil himself names not the holy and the good, but nature's power to procreate, to multiply life – in other words, Eros:

> *Der Luft, dem Wasser, wie der Erden*
> *Entwinden tausend Keime sich,*
> *Im Trocknen, Feuchten, Warmen, Kalten!*
> *Hätt' ich mir nicht die Flamme vorbehalten,*
> *Ich hätte nichts Aparts für mich.*

[From air, water and earth a thousand germs break forth, in dry, wet, warm and cold! Had I not reserved the flame for myself, I should have nothing to call my own.]

3. Our present view can be roughly expressed in the proposition that libido is involved in the manifestation of every drive, but not everything in this manifestation is libido.

4. Probably we should add, to be more precise: 'in the shape it was bound to take on after a certain event that is still a matter for conjecture'.

VII

Why do our relatives, the animals, show no sign of such a cultural struggle? We have no way of knowing. It is very likely that some of them – the bees, the ants, the termites – struggled for thousands of centuries until they evolved the state institutions, the distribution of functions, the restrictions on individuals, for which we admire them today. It is characteristic of our present condition that we feel we should not be happy in any of these animal states or the roles assigned in them to individuals. In the case of other animal species it may be that a temporary compromise was reached between the influences of their surroundings and the conflicting drives within them, so that any development was brought to a halt. It may be that in primitive man a fresh access of libido fanned fresh resistance on the part of the destructive drive. There are many questions to be asked, and as yet no answers.

Another question is closer to home. What means does civilization employ in order to inhibit the aggression it faces, to render it harmless and possibly eliminate it? We have already become acquainted with some of the methods, but not with the one that seems most important. We can study this in the development of the individual. What happens to him to render his aggressivity harmless? Something very curious, which we would not have suspected, but which is plain to see. The aggression is introjected, internalized, actually sent back to where it came from; in other words, it is directed against the individual's own ego. There it is taken over by a portion of the ego that sets itself up as the super-ego, in opposition to the rest, and is now prepared, as 'conscience', to exercise the same severe aggression against the ego that the latter would have liked to direct towards other individuals. The tension between the stern super-ego and the ego that is subject to it is what we call a 'sense of guilt'; this manifests itself as a need for punishment. In this way civilization overcomes the dangerous aggressivity of the individual, by weakening him, disarming him and setting up an internal authority to watch over him, like a garrison in a conquered town.

Regarding the origin of the sense of guilt, the analyst's view differs from that of other psychologists, and he too finds it difficult to account for. In the first place, if we ask how a person comes to have a sense of guilt, the answer we receive cannot be gainsaid: one feels guilty (pious people would say 'sinful') if one has done something one recognizes as 'evil'. Then we realize how little this tells us. After some hesitation we may add that even a person who has done no wrong, but merely recognizes in himself an intention to do wrong, may consider himself guilty – which raises the question of why in this case the intention is equated with the deed. Both cases presuppose that we have already recognized evil as reprehensible, as something that should not be carried out. How do we arrive at this judgement? We may reject the notion of an original – as it were, natural – capacity to distinguish between good and evil. Evil is often far from harmful or dangerous to the ego; it may even be something it welcomes and takes pleasure in. Here, then, is a pointer to an outside influence, which determines what is to be called good or evil. As a person's own feelings would not have led him in this direction, he must have a motive for submitting to this outside influence. This is easily dicovered in his helplessness and dependency on others; it can best be described as a fear of loss of love. If he loses the love of a person he depends on, he is no longer protected against various dangers; above all, he is exposed to the risk that this more powerful person will demonstrate his superiority by punishing him. At first, then, evil is something for which one is threatened with loss of love; it must therefore be avoided. Hence, it hardly matters whether one has already done something wrong or merely intends to; in either case the danger arises only if the supervising authority finds out, and in either case the authority would behave in the same way.

This state of mind we call a 'bad conscience', but it really does not merit the name, for at this stage consciousness of guilt is clearly no more than a fear of loss of love, a 'social' anxiety. In a small child it can never be anything else, but for many adults too the only change is that the place once occupied by the father, or by both parents, has been taken over by the wider human community. Hence, adults regularly allow themselves to commit wrongful acts that hold out the promise of enjoyment, so long as they are sure that the authority will not learn of it or cannot hold it against them; their only fear is of being found out.[1] This is the state of affairs that today's society generally has to reckon with.

Nothing much changes until the authority is internalized through the establishment of the super-ego. The phenomena of conscience are thereby raised to a new level; only now can one properly speak of conscience and a sense of guilt.[2] The fear of discovery is no longer an issue, nor is the difference between wrong-doing and the intention to do wrong, for nothing, not even one's thoughts, can be hidden from the super-ego. Of course, the real gravity of the situation has passed, for to the best of our belief the new authority, the super-ego, has no reason to ill-treat the ego, with which it is intimately linked. But the way it came into existence is still influential in ensuring the survival of what is past and has been surmounted, so that things remain essentially as they were at the beginning. The super-ego torments the sinful ego with the same anxieties and is on the look-out for opportunities to expose it to punishment by the external world.

At this second stage of development, the conscience exhibits a peculiarity that was absent at the first and is not easy to explain. The more virtuous a person is, the sterner and more distrustful is his conscience, so that the very people who have attained the highest degree of saintliness are in the end the ones who accuse themselves of being most sinful. Virtue thus forfeits part of its promised reward; the compliant and abstinent ego does not enjoy the trust of its mentor and seemingly strives in vain to earn it. Now, it will at once be objected that these are artificially contrived difficulties, that a stricter and more vigilant conscience is the hallmark of a moral nature, and that if saints call themselves sinners, this is not without justification, in view of the temptations they are under to satisfy their drives, temptations to which they are particularly exposed, as it is well known that temptations are only increased by constant frustration, but diminished, at least for a time, by the occasional satisfaction. Another fact in the highly problematic field of ethics is that ill luck – that is to say, external frustration – greatly enhances the force of conscience in the super-ego. So long as things go well for a person, his conscience is lenient and indulges the ego in all kinds of ways. When a misfortune has befallen him he searches his soul, recognizes his sinfulness, pitches the demands of his conscience higher, imposes privations on himself, and punishes himself by acts of penance.[3] Whole peoples have behaved like this and still do. However, this is easily explained by reference to the original infantile phase of the conscience, which is not abandoned after the introjection into the super-ego, but persists beside and behind it. Fate is seen as replacing parental authority; if one suffers misfortune, this is because one is no longer loved by this supreme power, and under the threat of such loss of love, one again bows to the virtual parental authority of the super-ego, which one was happy to ignore while one's luck held. This becomes especially clear if one takes a strictly religious view and sees fate only as the expression of the divine will. The people of Israel had thought of itself as God's favourite child, and when the great Father let one misfortune after another rain down upon His people, it never doubted this relationship with God or questioned His power and justice, but brought forth the prophets, who reproached it for its sinfulness, and created, from its consciousness of guilt, the exceedingly stern precepts of its priestly religion. It is curious how differently primitive man behaves. Having met with misfortune, he puts the blame not on himself, but on the fetish, which has clearly not done its duty, and whips it instead of punishing himself.

We thus know of two origins of the sense of guilt: one is fear of authority; the other, which came later, is fear of the super-ego. The former forces us to forgo the satisfaction of our drives; in addition to this, the latter insists on punishment, for the continuance of our forbidden desires cannot be hidden from the super-ego. We have also learnt how the severity of the super-ego – the requirements of conscience – can be understood. This severity simply perpetuates that of the external authority, which it supersedes and partly replaces. We now see how renunciation of the drives relates to consciousness of guilt. Initially this renunciation results from fear of the external authority; one renounces certain satisfactions in order to avoid losing its love. After renouncing them, one is, as it were, quits with the authority, and no sense of guilt should remain. Things are different, however, when it comes to fear of the super-ego. To renounce the drives is no longer enough, for the desire persists and cannot be concealed from the super-ego. Despite one's renunciation, then, a sense of guilt will arise, and this is a great economic disadvantage in the institution of the super-ego, or, one might say, in the formation of conscience. Renunciation of the drives no longer has a fully liberating effect; virtuous abstention is no longer rewarded by the assurance of love; the threat of external unhappiness – loss of love, and punishment at the hands of the external authority – has been exchanged for an enduring inner unhappiness, the tension generated by the consciousness of guilt.

These interrelations are at once so complicated and so important that, at the risk of repeating myself, I should like to tackle them from a different angle. The chronological sequence, then, would be as follows: first, renunciation of the drives, resulting from fear of aggression from the external authority (for this is what fear of the loss of love amounts to, love being a protection against this punitive aggression), then the setting up of the internal authority and the renunciation of the drives, resulting from fear of this authority, fear of conscience. In this second situation an evil deed is on a par with an evil intention; hence the consciousness of guilt and the need for punishment. The aggression of the conscience continues the aggression of the external authority. This much is probably already clear, but what room is left for the influence of misfortune – renunciation imposed from without – which reinforces the conscience, for the extraordinary severity of conscience that is found in the best and most tractable persons? We have already explained both these peculiarities of conscience, but we probably still have the impression that our explanations fail to go to the heart of the matter and leave some things unexplained. And here at last an idea comes in that belongs entirely to psychoanalysis and is foreign to our ordinary way of thinking. This idea is such as to enable us to understand why the subject was bound to strike us as so confused and lacking in transparency. For it tells us that although it is at first the conscience (or, rather, the fear that later becomes the conscience) that causes us to renounce the drives, this causal relation is later reversed. Every renunciation of the drives now becomes a dynamic source of conscience; every fresh renunciation reinforces its severity and intolerance; and if we could only bring it more into harmony with what we know about the emergence of conscience, we should be tempted to endorse the paradoxical statement that conscience results from the renunciation of the drives, or that this renunciation (imposed on us from without) creates the conscience, which then demands further renunciation.

The contradiction between this statement and what we have said about the genesis of the conscience is not so very great, and we can see a way of reducing it further. For greater ease of presentation let us take the example of the aggressive drive, and let us assume that we are dealing in every case with the renunciation of aggression. This is naturally to be taken only as a provisional assumption. The effect that the renunciation of the drives has on the conscience is such that any aggression whose satisfaction we forgo is taken over by the super-ego and increases the latter's aggression (towards the ego). This is not consistent with the view that the original aggression of the conscience continues the severity of the external authority and has therefore nothing to do with renunciation. The inconsistency is removed, however, if we assume a different origin for the super-ego's initial stock of aggression. A considerable measure of aggressivity must have developed in the child against the authority that deprives him of his first (and most significant) satisfactions, no matter what kind of deprivations were required. The child is obliged to forgo the satisfaction of this vengeful aggression. He helps himself out of this difficult economic situation by recourse to familiar mechanisms. By means of identification he incorporates this unassailable authority into himself; it now becomes the super-ego and takes over all the aggression that, as a child, one would have liked to exercise against it. The child's ego has to content itself with the sad role of the authority – the father – which has been so degraded. As so often happens, the original situation is reversed. 'If I were the father and you the child, I should treat you badly.' The relation between the super-ego and the ego amounts to the return, distorted by the subject's desire, of the real relations between the once undivided ego and an external object. This is typical too. The essential difference, however, is that the original severity of the super-ego is not – or not to such a great extent – the severity that one has experienced from him [the father] or attributes to him; it represents rather one's own aggression towards him. If this is correct, one can actually maintain that conscience initially arose through the suppression of an aggressive impulse and continues to be reinforced by similar suppressions.

Which of these two views is correct – the earlier one, which we found genetically incontestable, or the newer one, which rounds off the theory in such a welcome fashion? Clearly both are justified, as is shown by the evidence of direct observation. They do not contradict each other; they even coincide at one point, for the vengeful aggression of the child will be determined partly by the amount of punitive aggression he expects from his father. Experience teaches us, however, that the severity of the super-ego that is developed by a child in no way replicates the severity of the treatment he has himself experienced.[4] It appears to be independent of this: even with a very lenient upbringing, a child may develop a very stern conscience. Yet it would also be wrong to exaggerate this independence; it is not difficult to convince oneself that a strict upbringing also has a strong influence on the formation of the child's super-ego. This amounts to saying that, in the formation of the super-ego and the emergence of conscience, innate constitutional factors act in concert with influences from the real environment. This is not at all surprising; indeed, it is the universal aetiological condition for all such processes.[5]

One can also say that if a child reacts to the first great frustrations of the drives with excessive aggression and a corresponding severity of the super-ego, it is following a phylogenetic model and going beyond the reaction that would be justified today; for the primeval father was certainly terrible and could be credited with the utmost aggression. The differences between the two views of the genesis of conscience are thus reduced still further if one shifts one's attention from individual to phylogenetic development. On the other hand, we become aware of a new and significant difference between these two developmental processes. We cannot get away from the assumption that the sense of guilt stems from the Oedipus complex and was acquired when the brothers banded together and killed the father. On that occasion aggression was not suppressed, but acted out – the same aggression whose suppression in the child is supposed to be the source of his sense of guilt. At this point I should not be surprised if the exasperated reader were to exclaim, 'So it's immaterial whether one kills one's father or not – one acquires a sense of guilt in any case! Here one may take leave to voice a few doubts. Either it is not true that the sense of guilt derives from suppressed aggression, or else the whole story of the killing of the father is a fiction, and primeval children did not kill their fathers any more often than children do today. Besides, if it is not a fiction, but a plausible piece of history, it would be a case of something happening that everybody expects to happen – of someone feeling guilty because he really has done something that cannot be justified. And for such cases, which after all occur every day, psychoanalysis still owes us an explanation.'

This is true, and the matter must be remedied. Nor is there any great mystery about it. If one has a sense of guilt after committing a misdeed, and because one has committed it, this feeling ought rather to be called *remorse*. It relates only to a deed, although of course it presupposes that before the deed there was already a *conscience*, a readiness to feel guilty. Such remorse can therefore never help us to discover the origin of conscience and of the sense of guilt generally. What usually happens in these everyday cases is that a need generated by a drive acquires sufficient strength to prevail over a relatively weak conscience and achieve satisfaction; once satisfied, the need is naturally reduced, and the previous balance of forces is restored. Psychoanalysis is therefore right to exclude from the present discussion the case of a sense of guilt that stems from remorse, however common it is and however great its practical importance.

But if man's sense of guilt goes back to the killing of the primeval father, this too was a case of 'remorse'. So should we suppose that conscience and a sense of guilt did not exist before the deed was done? Where did the remorse come from in this case? Undoubtedly this case should clear up the mystery of the sense of guilt and put an end to our embarrassments. And I believe it does. This remorse was the result of the primordial emotional ambivalence towards the father: his sons hated him, but they also loved him. Once their hate was satisfied by this act of aggression, their love manifested itself in the remorse they felt for the deed. Through identification with the father, this love established the super-ego, endowed it with the power of the father – as though to punish the act of aggression committed against him – and invented restrictions that would prevent its repetition. And since aggressivity towards the father recurred in succeeding generations, the sense of guilt remained too, and was reinforced whenever aggression was suppressed and transferred to the super-ego. Now, I think, we can at last grasp two things quite clearly: the part played by love in the emergence of conscience and the fateful inevitability of the sense of guilt. Whether one has killed one's father or refrained from doing so is not really decisive; in either case one is bound to feel guilty, for the sense of guilt is the expression of the conflict of ambivalence, the unending struggle between Eros and the destructive drive, the death drive. This conflict is fanned as soon as people are faced with the task of living together. So long as the family is the only form of communal life, the conflict is bound to express itself in the Oedipus complex, to establish the conscience and to create the primordial sense of guilt. When an attempt is made to extend the community, the conflict is continued in forms that depend on the past; it is reinforced, and leads to an increased sense of guilt. Because civilization obeys an internal erotic impulse that requires it to unite human beings in a tightly knit mass, it can achieve this goal only by constantly reinforcing the sense of guilt. What began in relation to the father is brought to fruition in relation to the mass. If civilization is the necessary trend of development that leads from the family to humanity as a whole, it follows that the intensification of the sense of guilt, perhaps to a degree that the individual finds hard to endure, is indissolubly linked with it, as a consequence of the innate conflict of ambivalence, of the perpetual contention between love and the death-wish. One is reminded of the poet's poignant indictment of the 'heavenly powers':

> *Ihr führt ins Leben uns hinein,*
> *Ihr lasst den Armen schuldig werden,*
> *Dann überlasst ihr ihn der Pein,*
> *Denn jede Schuld rächt sich auf Erden.*[6]

[You lead us into life, you let the poor man become guilty, then you deliver him to punishment, for all guilt is avenged on earth.]

And one may well breathe a sigh of relief when one recognizes that it is nevertheless given to a few human beings to produce the most profound insights, more or less effortlessly, from the maelstrom of their own feelings, while we others constantly have to grope our way forward through agonizing insecurity.

Notes

1. Here one might recall Rousseau's famous mandarin!
2. Any perceptive person will understand and take into account the fact that the present synopsis makes sharp distinctions where the real transitions are more gradual, that it is not just a question of the existence of the super-ego, but of its relative strength and its sphere of influence. After all, what has so far been said about conscience and guilt is generally known and hardly disputed.
3. The part played by misfortune in the promotion of morality is the subject of a delightful short story by Mark Twain, *The first melon I ever stole*. This first melon chanced to be unripe. I heard Mark Twain read the story himself.

After reading out the title he stopped and asked himself: 'Was it the first?' That said it all: the first was not the only one. [This last sentence was added in 1931.]

4. As Melanie Klein and other English authors have rightly stressed.

5. In *Psychoanalyse der Gesamtpersönlichkeit* (1927) Franz Alexander has accurately assessed the two main types of pathogenic methods of upbringing, over-strictness and over-indulgence, in connection with Aichhorn's study of delinquency. The 'excessively soft and indulgent' father will cause a child to form an excessively severe super-ego, because the child, influenced by the love it receives, has no other way of dealing with its aggression than by turning it inwards. In the delinquent who has been brought up without love there is no tension between the ego and the super-ego: all his aggression can be directed outwards. Hence, if one disregards any constitutional factor that may be presumed to exist, one can say that a strict conscience arises from the interplay of two influences on a person's life: the frustration of the drives, which unleashes aggression, and the experience of being loved, which turns this aggression inwards and transfers it to the super-ego.

6. Song of the Harpist in Goethe's *Wilhelm Meister*.

VIII

Having reached the end of a road like the present one, the author must beg his readers' forgiveness for not being a more skilful guide and for not sparing them a number of dreary stretches and tiresome detours. It can undoubtedly be done better. I will now try, rather late in the day, to make some amends.

In the first place, I suspect, the readers will have the impression that the discussions of the sense of guilt distort the framework of this essay, in that they take up too much space and push the rest of the content, with which they are not always closely related, to one side. This may have disturbed the structure of the study, but accords entirely with its intention, which is to present the sense of guilt as the most important problem in the development of civilization and to show how the price we pay for cultural progress is a loss of happiness, arising from a heightened sense of guilt.[1]

Whatever still seems strange about this proposition, the final conclusion of our study, can probably be traced back to the quite peculiar relationship, which still is far from understood, between the sense of guilt and our consciousness. In the common instances of remorse that we regard as normal, the sense of guilt makes itself clearly perceptible to the consciousness; indeed, we often speak of a 'consciousness of guilt' instead of a 'sense of guilt'. From the study of neuroses, to which, after all, we owe the most valuable pointers to an understanding of what is normal, a number of contradictions emerge. In one of these disorders, obsessional neurosis, the sense of guilt forces itself stridently on the consciousness, dominating both the clinical picture and the patient's life, and allowing hardly anything else to appear beside it. In most other forms of neurosis, however, it remains quite unconscious, though the effects it produces are not for that reason any less important. Patients do not believe us when we tell them they have an 'unconscious sense of guilt', and so, to make ourselves to some extent intelligible, we speak of an unconscious need for punishment, in which the sense of guilt expresses itself. However, its connection with one form of neurosis should not be overstated, for even in cases of obsessional neurosis there are some types of patient who are unaware of their sense of guilt, or who experience it only as a tormenting *malaise*, a kind of anxiety, when they are prevented from carrying out certain actions. One day we should be able to understand these things, but at present we cannot. At this point it might be useful to remark that the sense of guilt is fundamentally nothing other than a topical variety of anxiety; in its later phases it merges completely with *fear of the super-ego*. In the case of anxiety too we find the same extraordinary variations in its relation to consciousness. It is present in some way behind all the symptoms, though sometimes it seizes control of the whole of the consciousness, while at other times it is completely hidden, so that we have to speak of an unconscious anxiety or – if we wish to retain a clear psychological conscience, anxiety being initially only a feeling – of 'possibilities of anxiety'. Hence, it is quite conceivable that even the sense of guilt engendered by civilization is not recognized as such, but remains for the most part unconscious, or manifests itself as an unease, a discontent, for which other motivations are sought. The religions, at least, have never ignored the part that a sense of guilt plays in civilization. Moreover – a point I failed to appreciate earlier[2] – they claim to redeem humanity from this sense of guilt, which they call sin. From the way in which this redemption is achieved in Christianity – through the sacrificial death of one man, who thereby takes upon himself the guilt shared by all – we drew an inference as to what may have been the original occasion for our acquiring this primordial guilt, which also marked the beginning of civilization.[3]

It cannot be very important, though it may not be entirely superfluous, to elucidate the meanings of a few terms such as 'super-ego', 'conscience', 'sense of guilt', 'need for punishment' and 'remorse', which may often have been used too loosely and interchangeably. They all apply to the same relationship, while denoting different aspects of it. The super-ego is an authority that we postulate, and conscience a function that we ascribe to it, along with others – this function being to supervise and assess the actions and intentions of the ego, to exercise a kind of censorship. The sense of guilt, the harshness of the super-ego, is thus identical with the severity of the conscience; it is the ego's perception of being supervised in this way, its assessment of the tension between its own strivings and the claims of the super-ego. Fear of this critical authority – a fear that underlies the whole relationship and amounts to a need for punishment – is the manifestation of a drive on the part of the ego, which has become masochistic under the influence of the sadistic super-ego and devotes a portion of its inherent drive for internal destruction to establishing an erotic bond with the super-ego. One should not speak of conscience until the super-ego can be shown to exist. As for the sense of guilt, one has to admit that it predates the super-ego, and therefore the conscience. At this early stage it is a direct manifestation of the fear of external authority, an acknowledgement of the tension between the ego and this authority, a direct derivative of the conflict between the need for its love and the urge for the satisfaction of the drives, the inhibiting of which generates aggressivity. The superimposition of the two layers of the sense of guilt – the one due to fear of the external authority, the other to fear of the internal authority – has greatly hampered our understanding of the relations that the conscience enters into. Remorse is a general term for the reaction of the ego in cases that involve a sense of guilt; it contains, in largely unaltered form, the emotional material of the anxiety that is at work behind the sense of guilt. It is itself a punishment and may involve the need for punishment. Thus it too may pre-date conscience.

Nor can there be any harm in reviewing the contradictions that have temporarily confused us in the course of our investigation. At one point it was said that the sense of guilt resulted from an act of aggression that had *not* been carried out, while at another – and precisely at its historical inception, the killing of the father – it was said to derive from one that *had* been. We managed to find a way out of this difficulty. With the institution of the internal authority, the super-ego, the situation changed radically. Before this, the sense of guilt had been identical with remorse, a term that should properly be reserved for the reaction that follows the acting out of aggression. After this, thanks to the omniscient super-ego, the distinction between intended and fulfilled aggression lost its force. A sense of guilt might now result not only from a violent deed that was actually performed – as everyone knows – but also from one that was merely intended – as psychoanalysis has discovered. Despite the new psychological situation, the conflict of ambivalence between the two primal drives still produces the same effect. There is an obvious temptation to seek here the solution of the problem posed by the varying relation of the sense of guilt to consciousness. A sense of guilt that arises from remorse for an evil *deed* should always be conscious, whereas one that is prompted by the perception of an evil *impulse* might remain unconscious. Yet it is not as simple as that: obsessional neurosis emphatically contradicts this view. The second contradiction was that, according to one view, the aggressive energy that we ascribe to the super-ego merely perpetuates the punitive energy of the external authority and preserves it in the mind, whereas according to another view it is one's own unused aggression, directed against this inhibiting authority. The former view seems to accord more with the history, the latter more with the theory of the sense of guilt. Detailed consideration has succeeded almost too well in resolving this apparently irreconcilable contradiction; what remains as the essential common factor is that both involve internalized aggression. Again, clinical observation actually allows us to distinguish between the two sources of aggression that we ascribe to the super-ego, but in any given case either the one or the other may produce the stronger effect, though as a rule they act in concert.

This is, I think, an appropriate place at which to enter a serious plea for a view whose provisional acceptance we recommended a short while back. In the latest analytic literature we find a predilection for the view that the sense of guilt is, or may be, intensified by any kind of frustration – if satisfaction of any drive is thwarted.[4] I think we gain a substantial theoretical simplification if we take this to apply only to the *aggressive* drives. Little will be found to conflict with this assumption. For how are we to explain, dynamically and economically, a heightening of the sense of guilt that appears when there is an unsatisfied *erotic* demand? This seems possible, after all, only if we presume a circuitous route – if the prevention of erotic satisfaction provokes aggressivity towards whoever interferes with it, and if this aggressivity then has to be suppressed. But then only the aggression is converted into a sense of guilt by being suppressed and transferred to the super-ego. I am convinced that we shall be able to represent many processes more simply and transparently if the findings of psychoanalysis relating to the origin of the sense of guilt are restricted to the aggressive drives. In this case, examination of the clinical material does not yield an unambiguous answer: in accordance with our hypothesis, the two kinds of drive almost never appear in their pure form, mutually isolated. However, a study of extreme cases will no doubt point in the direction I anticipate. It is tempting to derive an initial advantage from this more restricted view by applying it to the process of repression. As we have discovered, the symptoms of neuroses are essentially substitutive satisfactions for unfulfilled sexual desires. In our analytic work we have been surprised to find that perhaps every neurosis conceals a certain measure of unconscious guilt, and this in turn intensifies the symptoms by using them as a punishment. It now seems plausible to formulate the following proposition: when a drive is repressed, its libidinal elements are converted into symptoms and its aggressive components into a sense of guilt. Even if this thesis only approximates to the truth, it still merits our interest.

Some readers may feel that they have heard the formula of the struggle between Eros and the death drive too often. It was meant to characterize both the cultural process undergone by humanity and the development undergone by the individual; moreover, it was said to have revealed the secret of organic life in general. It seems imperative to investigate how these three processes relate to one another. Now, the recurrence of the formula is justified as soon as one considers that the development of human civilization and the development of the individual are both vital processes and must therefore partake of the nature of life in the most general sense. On the other hand, the very universality of this feature means that proof of its presence is of no help in differentiating these processes, unless it is narrowed down by particular conditions. Hence, we can be content only with the statement that the process of civilization is a special modification of the life process that is undergone by the latter under the influence of a task that is set by Eros at the instigation of Ananke (the exigency of reality) – the task of uniting discrete individuals in a community bound together by libidinal ties. However, if we focus our attention on the relation between the civilization of mankind and the development or upbringing of the individual, we shall conclude, without much hesitation, that the two processes are very similar in kind, if not indeed one and the same process, as it affects different kinds of object. Human civilization naturally belongs to a higher order of abstraction than the development of the individual; it is therefore harder to apprehend in concrete terms, and the search for analogies should not be compulsively pursued to excess. Yet in view of the similarity of the aims – the one being to create a unified mass consisting of many individuals, the other to integrate the individual into such a mass – the similarity of the means used in the two processes and the similarity of the resultant phenomena will come as no surprise. There is one distinction between the two processes that is of such extraordinary significance that it must not remain unmentioned any longer. In the development of the individual, the programme of the pleasure principle, aimed at the attainment of happiness, remains paramount. Integration into a community, or adaptation to it, seems a scarcely avoidable condition; it has to be met if the goal of happiness is to be reached. Perhaps it would be better if this were possible without such a condition. In other words, the development of the individual seems to be a product of the interaction of two trends – the striving for happiness, which we commonly call 'egoistic', and the striving for fellowship within the community, which we call 'altruistic'. Neither term goes much below the surface. In the development of the individual, as we have said, the emphasis falls mostly on the egoistic striving for happiness, while the other process, which we may call 'cultural', is usually content with a restrictive role. In the process of civilization things are different: the aim of forming a unified whole out of individual human beings is all-important. True, the aim of happiness is still present, but it is pushed into the background; it is almost as though the creation of a great human community would be most successful if there were no need for concern with individual happiness. There may thus be particular features in the development of the individual that are not matched in the process of civilization; the former need coincide with the latter only in so far as its aim is to incorporate the individual into the community.

Just as the planet still circles round its sun, yet at the same time rotates on its own axis, so the individual partakes in the development of humanity while making his own way through life. To our dull gaze, however, the play of forces in the heavens seems frozen in a changeless order, while in the field of organic life we can still see how the forces contend with one another, and how the conflict yields ever-changing results. In the same way the two strivings – for individual happiness and for human fellowship – have to contend with each other in every individual; so too the processes of individual and cultural development are bound to come into conflict and dispute each other's territory. But this struggle between the individual and society does not derive from the no doubt irreconcilable antagonism of the primal drives, Eros and death; it indicates a conflict in the economy of the libido, which may be compared with the conflict regarding the distribution of the libido between the ego and its objects. It admits of an eventual accommodation within the individual, such as we may hope for in the future of civilization, however oppressive it may be at present in the life of the individual.

The analogy between the development of civilization and that of the individual can be significantly extended. One can justifiably maintain that the community too evolves a super-ego and that the development of civilization takes place under its influence. Anyone who is conversant with different civilizations may find it tempting to pursue this equation in detail. I will confine myself to drawing attention to a few striking points. The super-ego of a cultural epoch has an origin not unlike that of the individual; it rests upon the impression left behind by the personalities of great leaders, people who were endowed with immense spiritual or intellectual power or in whom some human striving found its strongest and purest, and hence often most one-sided, expression. In many cases the analogy goes even further, in that in their lifetime these figures were quite often, though not always, mocked and abused by others, or even cruelly done to death – just as indeed the primeval father did not attain divinity until long after he was done to death. The most poignant example of this fateful link is the figure of Jesus Christ – unless this figure is mythological and was called into being on the basis of an obscure memory of that primeval event. A further point of agreement is that both the cultural and the individual super-ego make stern ideal demands, and that failure to meet these demands is punished by 'fear of conscience'. Here, indeed, we encounter a curious phenomenon: the relevant mental processes, when seen in the mass, are more familiar, more accessible to our consciousness than they can ever be in the individual. In the individual only the aggression of the super-ego makes itself clearly heard, when tension arises, in the form of reproaches, while the demands themselves often remain unconscious in the background. When brought fully into consciousness, they are seen to coincide with the precepts of the current cultural super-ego. At this point there seems to be a regular cohesion, as it were, between the cultural development of the mass and the personal development of the individual. Some manifestations and properties of the super-ego can thus be recognized more easily by its behaviour in the cultural community than by its behaviour in the individual.

After developing its ideals, the cultural super-ego sets up its demands. Among these, the demands concerned with the mutual relations of human beings are collectively known as ethics. A high value has always been placed on ethics, as though it were expected to perform exceptionally important services. And indeed it does address itself to the subject that is easily recognized as the sorest point in any civilization. Ethics is thus to be viewed as an attempt at therapy, an endeavour to achieve, through a precept of the super-ego, what has not so far been achievable through other cultural activities. As we know, the problem is how to remove the greatest obstacle to civilization, the constitutional propensity of human beings to mutual aggression, and for this very reason we have a special interest in what is probably the most recent commandment of the cultural super-ego: 'Love thy neighbour as thyself.' The study and treatment of neuroses lead us to level two reproaches against the individual super-ego: in the severity of its precepts and prohibitions it shows too little concern for the happiness of the ego, in that it fails to take sufficient account of the forces that oppose compliance with them, the instinctual strength of the id, and the difficulties that prevail in the real environment. For therapeutic purposes we are therefore often obliged to oppose the super-ego and attempt to lower its demands. We can make quite similar objections to the ethical demands of the cultural super-ego. This too is insufficiently concerned with the facts of man's psychical constitution; it issues a commandment without asking whether it can be obeyed. It assumes that it is psychologically possible for the human ego to do whatever is required of it, that the ego has absolute control over the id. This is an error. Even in people who are called normal, control of the id cannot be increased beyond certain limits. To demand more is to provoke the individual to rebellion or neurosis, or to make him unhappy. The commandment 'Love thy neighbour as thyself' is the strongest defence against human aggression and an excellent example of the unpsychological manner in which the cultural super-ego proceeds. It is impossible to keep this commandment; such a huge inflation of love can only lower its value, not remove the problem. Civilization neglects all this; it reminds us only that the harder it is to comply with a precept, the more merit there is in compliance. Yet in today's civilization, whoever adheres to such a precept puts himself at a disadvantage in relation to all who flout it. How potent an obstacle to civilization aggression must be if the defence against it can cause as much unhappiness as the aggression itself! In this situation, what we call natural ethics has nothing to offer but the narcissistic satisfaction of being able to think one is better than others. This is where ethics based on religion enters the scene with its promises of a better life hereafter. I am inclined to think that, for as long as virtue goes unrewarded here below, ethics will preach in vain. I have no doubt, too, that a real change in people's relations to property will be of more help here than any ethical commandment; yet the recognition of this fact among socialists has been obscured and made impracticable by a new idealistic misreading of human nature.

An approach that tries to trace the role of a super-ego in the phenomena of cultural development seems to me to promise further discoveries. I must hasten to a close, but there is still one question I can hardly avoid. If the development of civilization so much resembles that of the individual and operates with the same means, is one not entitled to proffer the diagnosis that some civilizations or cultural epochs – possibly the whole of humanity – have become 'neurotic' under the influence of cultural strivings? The analytic dissection of these neuroses might be followed up by suggestions for therapy that would merit great interest. I could not say that such an attempt to apply psychoanalysis to the cultural community would be absurd or doomed to futility. But one would have to be very cautious, remembering that one was dealing only with analogies, and that with concepts, as with human beings, it is dangerous to wrench them out of the sphere in which they originated and have evolved. Moreover, the diagnosis of communal neuroses comes up against a special difficulty: in the individual neurosis the first clue we have is the contrast between the patient and his supposedly normal environment. When it comes to a mass of individuals, all affected by the same condition, no such background is present; it would have to be borrowed from elsewhere. And as for the therapeutic application of the knowledge one obtained, of what use would even the most apposite analysis of a social neurosis be, if no one had the authority to force the mass to undergo treatment? Yet despite all these difficulties we may be fairly sure that one day somebody will venture upon such a pathological study of cultural communities.

For a variety of reasons I have no wish whatever to offer an evaluation of human civilization. I have been careful to refrain from the enthusiastic prejudice that sees our civilization as the most precious thing we possess or can acquire, and believes that its path will necessarily lead us to heights of perfection hitherto undreamt of. I can at least listen, without bridling, to the critic who thinks that, considering the goals of cultural endeavour and the means it employs, one is bound to conclude that the whole effort is not worth the trouble and can only result in a state of affairs that the individual is bound to find intolerable. My impartiality is facilitated by my scant knowledge of such matters. There is only one thing that I know for certain: the value judgements of human beings are undoubtedly guided by their desire for happiness and thus amount to an attempt to back up their illusions with arguments. I should understand perfectly if someone were to stress the inevitability of human civiliz- ation and maintain, for instance, that the tendency to restrict sexual life, or to promote the humanitarian ideal at the expense of natural selection, were trends that could not be averted or deflected and that it was best to yield to them as if they were naturally ordained. On the other hand, I am familiar with the objection that in the course of human history such strivings, which we consider insurmountable, have often been cast aside and replaced by others. I therefore dare not set myself up as a prophet *vis-à-vis* my fellow men, and I plead guilty to the reproach that I cannot bring them any consolation, which is fundamentally what they all demand, the wildest revolution- aries no less passionately than the most well-behaved and pious believers.

The fateful question for the human race seems to be whether, and to what extent, the development of its civilization will manage to overcome the disturbance of communal life caused by the human drive for aggression and self-destruction. Perhaps in this context the present age is worthy of special interest. Human beings have made such strides in controlling the forces of nature that, with the help of these forces, they will have no difficulty in exterminating one another, down to the last man. They know this, and it is this know- ledge that accounts for much of their present disquiet, unhappiness and anxiety. And now it is to be expected that the other of the two 'heavenly powers', immortal Eros, will try to assert himself in the struggle with his equally immortal adversary. But who can foresee the outcome?[5]

(1930)

Notes

1. 'Thus conscience doth make cowards of us all . . .' That a modern upbringing conceals from the young person the role that sexuality will play in his life is not the only criticism that must be levelled against it. Another of its sins is that it does not prepare him for the aggression of which he is destined to be the object. To send the young out into life with such a false psychological orientation is like equipping people who are setting out on a polar expedition with summer clothes and maps of the North Italian lakes. This reveals a certain misuse of ethical demands. The severity of these would do little harm if the educators said, 'This is how people ought to be if they are to be happy and make others happy, but one must reckon with their not being like this.' Instead, the young person is led to believe that everyone else complies with these ethical precepts and is therefore virtuous. This is the basis of the requirement that he too should become virtuous.

2. I refer to *Die Zukunft einer Illusion* [*The Future of an Illusion*] (1927) [I] (*Gesammelte Werke*, vol. XIV).

3. *Totem und Tabu* [*Totem and Taboo*] [VI.6] (*Gesammelte Werke*, vol. IX).

4. Especially in the contributions of E. Jones, Susan Isaacs and Melanie Klein, and also, I understand, of Reik and Alexander.

5. [This last sentence was added in 1931.]

*'Civilized' Sexual Morality
and Modern Nervous Illness*

In his recently published work *Sexualethik*[1] Christian von Ehrenfels dwells at some length on the distinction between 'natural' and 'civilized' sexual morality. By natural sexual morality we are to understand one under whose dominance a community can sustain itself in health and vitality, while civilized sexual morality is one whose observance spurs human beings on to intense and productive cultural activity. According to Ehrenfels the difference between them is brought out most clearly when a people's *constitutive* properties are set against its *cultural* assets. For further consideration of this significant train of thought I refer the reader to Ehrenfels's work itself; here I will take from it only what I need as a starting point for my own contribution.

It is an obvious assumption that under the dominance of a civilized sexual morality the health and fitness of individuals will be subject to certain impairments, and that the harm they suffer from the sacrifices imposed on them will eventually reach such a pitch as to put the ultimate cultural aim indirectly at risk. Indeed, Ehrenfels relates a number of ill effects to the sexual morality that prevails in present-day western society, effects for which he is bound to hold it responsible, and, while fully acknowledging its great aptitude for the promotion of civilization, he is obliged to condemn it as being in need of reform. Characteristic features of the civilized sexual morality that dominates us are for him the extension of the demands made on women to the sexual life of men and the prohibition of any sexual intercourse outside monogamous wedlock. Of course, regard for the natural differences between the sexes makes it necessary to punish men's lapses less rigorously, and so to admit a *double standard* for them. Yet a society that entertains such a double standard cannot carry 'love of truth, honesty and humanity' beyond a certain narrow limit;[2] it cannot help teaching its members to cloak the truth, to gloss over things, and to deceive themselves and others. Civilized sexual morality produces still more harmful effects by glorifying monogamy and thus paralysing the factor of *virile selection*, through whose influence alone, according to Ehrenfels, constitutional improvement is to be achieved, since in civilized nations *vital selection* is reduced to a minimum by humanity and hygiene.[3]

Now, among the harmful effects that are laid at the door of civilized sexual morality the physician misses the very one whose importance will be discussed in detail here. I refer to its role in promoting modern nervous illness – that is to say, the kind of nervous illness that is rapidly spreading in today's society. Every so often a patient suffering from a nervous disorder will himself draw the doctor's attention to the part played in its causation by the conflict between the individual's constitution and the demands of civilization. He may say, for instance: 'In our family we've all become nervous because we've wanted to be something better than we can be, given our background.' And often enough the doctor is given pause for thought when he observes that those who succumb to nervous illness are the offspring of fathers who, coming from rough but vigorous families, and having been reared in simple, healthy rural conditions, make a triumphal entry into the big city and before long enable their children to rise to a high level of civilization. Yet it is above all the nerve specialists themselves who have proclaimed the link between the 'growth of nervous illness' and modern civilized living. Let us illustrate the reasons they advance for this connection by a few excerpts from statements made by distinguished observers.

W. Erb:[4] 'The question originally posed, then, is whether the causes of nervous illness that have been presented to you are so much more widespread in modern life as to explain the increase in this kind of illness – and this is a question that can no doubt be answered unhesitatingly in the affirmative, as a brief glance at modern living and the factors that shape it will show.

'One thing emerges clearly from a number of general facts: the extraordinary achievements of modern times, the discoveries and inventions in every sphere, and the maintenance of progress in the face of growing competition, have been achieved – and can be maintained – only by great mental effort. The demands made on the individual's efficiency in the struggle for existence have increased substantially, and he can satisfy them only by summoning up all his mental energies. At the same time the individual's needs have grown; demands for the enjoyment of life have increased in all strata of society, and a degree of luxury hitherto unknown has spread to classes that were previously untouched by it. Irreligion, discontent and covetousness have proliferated in broad sections of the population. The enormous expansion of communications, due to the world-wide telegraph and telephone networks, has entirely transformed the conditions of trade and commerce. Everything is done in haste, at fever pitch. The night is used for travel, the day for business; even "holiday trips" put a strain on the nervous system. Great political, industrial and financial crises carry this excitement into far wider areas of the population than ever before. Interest in political life has become universal: tempers are inflamed by political, religious and social struggles, party politics, electioneering and the immense growth of trade-unionism; people are forced to engage in constant mental activity and robbed of the time they need for relaxation, sleep and rest. Big-city life has become increasingly sophisticated and restless. The exhausted nerves seek recuperation in increased stimulation, in highly spiced pleasures, and the result is even greater exhaustion. Modern literature deals predominantly with the most ticklish problems, which stir up all the passions and encourage sensuality, hedonism, and contempt for all ethical principles and ideals. The reader is presented with pathological characters and with subjects that involve psychopathic sexuality, revolution and other problems. Our ears are excited and over-stimulated by large doses of noisy, obtrusive music. Theatres captivate all the senses with their sensational productions. Even the plastic arts turn by preference to the repulsive, the ugly and the exciting, and do not hesitate to place before our eyes, with revolting realism, the most hideous sights that reality has to offer.

'This general picture thus illustrates some of the dangers in the evolution of our modern civilization. Let me supplement it by a few details.'

Binswanger:[5] 'Neurasthenia in particular has been called an altogether modern disease, and Beard, to whom we owe the first comprehensive account of it, thought he had discovered a new nervous disease that had emerged on American soil. This assumption was of course mistaken, but the fact that it should have been an *American* clinician who was first able, on the basis of extensive experience, to grasp and record the peculiar features of this sickness probably indicates its close links with modern life, with the tireless, unbridled pursuit of money and possessions, and with the immense advances in applied science that have made any temporal or spatial obstacles to communications illusory.'

Krafft-Ebing:[6] 'The lives of countless civilized human beings now exhibit a host of anti-hygienic factors, which makes it easy to understand the alarming spead of nervous disease, for these harmful elements affect the brain first and foremost. The last few decades have seen great changes in the political and social conditions of civilized nations, especially in their mercantile, industrial and agrarian conditions. These changes have substantially affected professional life, one's status as a citizen, and one's possessions – and all at the expense of the nervous system, which has to contend with increased social and economic demands through a greater expenditure of energy, often with insufficient relaxation.'

My objection to these and many other similar-sounding doctrines is not that they are wrong, but that they prove inadequate when it comes to clarifying the details of nervous disorders and that they take no account of the most significant factor in the aetiology of these disorders. If one disregards the more indeterminate ways of being 'nervous' and looks at the real forms of nervous illness, the baleful influence of civilization is reduced essentially to the harmful suppression of sexual life in civilized peoples (or classes) by the 'civilized' sexual morality prevailing in them.

I have tried to supply the proof of this view in a series of specialist papers;[7] I cannot repeat it here, but I will cite the main arguments contained in my studies.

Precise clinical observation entitles us to distinguish between two groups of nervous conditions: *neuroses* proper and *psychoneuroses*. In the former, the disturbances (symptoms) – whether they manifest themselves in physical or mental functions – appear to be of a *toxic* nature, in that they behave quite like the phenomena associated with an excessive supply of certain nerve toxins or a lack of them. Now, these neuroses, which are usually grouped together as 'neurasthenia', can be generated by certain harmful influences in the subject's sexual life, without necessarily being aided by a hereditary taint; indeed, the form of the illness corresponds to the nature of these harmful factors, so that often enough the clinical picture can be used without further ado in order to deduce the particular sexual causation *a posteriori*. On the other hand, there is no evidence of any such regular correspondence between the form of the nervous disorder and the other harmful effects of civilization to which the writers have attributed it. We can therefore state that the sexual factor is essential in the aetiology of neuroses proper.

In the case of psychoneuroses the hereditary influence is more significant and the causation less transparent. However, a special investigative procedure known as psychoanalysis has enabled us to see that the symptoms of these disorders (hysteria, obsessional neurosis and so forth) are *psychogenic* and dependent on the operation of unconscious (repressed) complexes of ideas. The same method has familiarized us with these unconscious complexes too and shown that – to put it in quite general terms – they have a sexual content, springing from the needs of those who are sexually unsatisfied and representing for them a kind of substitute satisfaction. Hence, any factors that impair sexual life, that suppress its activity and displace its aims, must be regarded as pathogenic factors in the psychoneuroses too.

The value of the theoretical distinction between toxic and psychogenic neuroses is of course not vitiated by the fact that in most neurotic subjects one can observe disturbances that are traceable to both sources.

Now, anyone who is prepared to join with me in seeking the causation of nervous illness principally in harmful influences on the patient's sexual life will also wish to follow the ensuing discussions, which are intended to set the problem of growing nervous illness within a more general context.

In quite general terms, our civilization is built on the suppression of our drives. Every individual has surrendered part of what is properly his, a portion of his unrestricted authority, some of the aggressive and vindictive inclinations of his personality; it is these contributions by individuals that make up the common cultural heritage of material and non-material possessions. Apart from the exigencies of life, what has persuaded individuals to surrender so much is probably the family feeling that derives from eroticism. This renunciation has been progressive throughout the evolution of civilization. The single steps by which it has proceeded have been sanctioned by religion; any instinctual satisfaction that was renounced was offered to the deity, and the common property acquired in this way was declared to be 'holy'. Anyone whose constitution is so unbending as to be unable to suppress his drives confronts society as a 'criminal', an 'outlaw'[8] – unless his social position and outstanding abilities allow him to assert himself within society as a great man, a 'hero'.

The sex drive – or, more correctly, the sex drives, for analytic research shows that the sex drive is made up of a number of components or partial drives – is probably more highly developed in human beings than in most of the higher animals. It is at any rate more constant, having almost completely overcome the periodicity to which it is subject in animals. It puts huge amounts of energy at the disposal of cultural activity; this is a consequence of one particularly marked characteristic – its ability to shift its aim without any great loss of intensity. This capacity to exchange the originally sexual aim for another – which is no longer sexual but psychically related to the first – is called the capacity for *sublimation*. In contrast to this ability to shift its aims, which constitutes its value for civilization, the sex drive may also exhibit a particularly obdurate fixation, robbing it of its usefulness and causing it at times to degenerate into so-called abnormalities. The original strength of the sex drive no doubt differs from individual to individual; there is certainly some variation in the proportion of it that lends itself to sublimation. We imagine that in the first place it is the individual's constitution that determines how much of his sex drive can be sublimated and utilized. Moreover, the effects of experience and the influences that bear upon his mental apparatus may lead to the sublimation of a further portion of the drive. Yet there is a limit to this process of displacement, just as there is a limit to the conversion of heat into mechanical energy in our machines. For the great majority of constitutions a certain degree of direct sexual satisfaction seems indispensable, and the denial of this degree of satisfaction, which varies from individual to individual, entails the generation of phenomena that we are bound to regard as pathological because of the detriment they do to normal functions and the unpleasurable feelings they give rise to.

Further prospects open up when we consider the fact that the human sex drive does not originally serve the purposes of reproduction at all, but that its aim is to obtain particular kinds of pleasure.[9] This is how it manifests itself in childhood, when it derives pleasure not only from the genitals, but from other parts of the body (the erogenous zones) and can therefore disregard any objects other than these convenient ones. This stage we call the stage of *auto-eroticism*, and the task of restricting it is assigned to the child's upbringing, for if there were no progress beyond this stage, the sex drive would later become uncontrollable and unusable. The development of the sex drive thus proceeds from auto-eroticism to object-love, and from the autonomy of the erogenous zones to their subordination to the primacy of the genitals, which are then placed in the service of reproduction. During this development, a part of the sexual excitation produced by one's own body is inhibited, since it serves no reproductive end, and in favourable cases it is directed towards sublimation. In this way, those forces that can be employed in the service of civilization are obtained to a great extent through the suppression of the so-called *perverse* components of sexual excitation.

Given this account of the evolution of the sex drive, one might distinguish three stages of civilization: an initial stage, at which the the sex drive is free to range beyond the aim of reproduction; a second, at which everything belonging to the sex drive is suppressed except whatever serves this aim; and a third, at which only legitimate reproduction is permitted as a sexual aim. This third stage is represented by today's 'civilized' sexual morality.

If the second stage is taken as the norm, it must be noted, in the first place, that by reason of their constitutions a number of people cannot meet its demands. In whole classes of individuals the development we have described above – from auto-eroticism to object-love, with the aim of genital union – has not taken place correctly or not thoroughly enough. These developmental disturbances give rise to two species of harmful deviation from normal sexuality, from the kind of sexuality that furthers civilization; the two relate to each other almost as positive and negative. The people concerned are in the first place – if we disregard those who have an excessive sex drive that is altogether uninhibitable – the different types of *perverts*, in whom an infantile fixation on a provisional sexual aim has obstructed the primacy of the reproductive function, and *homosexuals* or *inverts*, for whom, in a manner that has not yet been fully clarified, the sexual aim has been deflected from the opposite sex. If these two kinds of developmental disturbance prove less injurious than one might have expected, this mitigation can be ascribed to the very make-up of the sex drive, which is highly complex and can make it possible for a person's sexual life to take on a serviceable final form, even when one or more of its components have failed to develop. Indeed, the constitution of those who are subject to inversion – the homosexuals – is often characterized by a special aptitude of the sex drive for cultural sublimation.

More pronounced forms of the perversions and of homosexuality, especially when they are exclusive, admittedly make their subjects socially useless and unhappy, so that even the demands of civilization at the second stage have to be recognized as a source of suffering for a certain proportion of humanity. The fate of the sufferers, who are constitutionally different from others, varies according to whether their innate sex drive is strong or relatively weak. Where the sex drive is generally weak, the victims of perversion can succeed in totally suppressing those proclivities that bring them into conflict with the moral demands of their stage of civilization. Yet from an ideal point of view this remains their only success, since in order to suppress their sex drives they consume those energies that they would otherwise direct towards cultural activity. They are, as it were, both inwardly inhibited and outwardly paralysed. What we shall repeat later on about the abstinence required of men and women at the third stage of civilization applies to them too.

If the sex drive is fairly intense, but perverted, two outcomes are possible. The first, which we will not consider further, is that the subjects remain perverted and have to bear the consequences of their deviation from the civilized standard. Far more interesting is the second outcome: in this case the perverted drives are admittedly suppressed, in accordance with upbringing and the requirements of society, but it is a kind of suppression that is really nothing of the sort and is better described as a suppression that has gone wrong. The inhibited sex drives, it is true, do not express themselves as such: herein lies the success. However, they do express themselves in other ways, which are just as harmful to the individual and render him just as useless to society as the unmodified satisfaction of the suppressed drives would have done: herein lies the failure of the process, which in the long run more than counterbalances its success. The substitutive phenomena that arise in the wake of the suppression of the drives amount to what we describe as nervous illness, more specifically as psychoneuroses (see the opening remarks above). Neurotics are that class of people who, because of a recalcitrant constitution, can achieve no more, under the influence of cultural requirements, than an *apparent* suppression of their drives, which becomes increasingly unsuccessful, and who for this reason can sustain their role in cultural activities only by dint of a great expenditure of energy and at the cost of inward impoverishment, or are periodically obliged to give it up and fall ill. However, I described the neuroses as the 'negative' of the perversions because in them the perverse impulses, after being repressed, appear from the unconscious part of the mind – because the neuroses contain, in a 'repressed' state, the same proclivities as the positive perversions.

Experience teaches us that for most people there is a limit beyond which their constitution cannot comply with the demands of civilization. All who seek to be nobler than their constitution permits succumb to neurosis; they would have been better in health if they had found it possible to be morally worse. The conclusion that perversion and neurosis relate to each other as positive and negative is often corroborated quite unequivocally by observations made within the same generation. Among siblings the brother may be a sexual pervert, while his sister, being a woman and endowed with a weaker sex drive, is a neurotic, though her symptoms express the same inclinations as the perversions of her sexually more active brother. And so in many families the men are healthy, but immoral to a socially undesirable extent, while the women are high-minded and excessively refined, but severely neurotic.

It is a glaring social injustice that civilized standards require us all to conduct our sex lives in the same way, even though some, thanks to their constitution, can do so effortlessly, while others have to endure the heaviest psychical sacrifices. Admittedly, this injustice is usually cancelled out by a failure to comply with moral prescriptions.

Up to now we have considered only the requirements of our postulated second stage of civilization, under which any so-called perverted sexual activity is prohibited, while 'normal' sexual intercourse is permitted. We have seen that, even with this distribution of sexual freedom and restriction, a number of individuals are pushed aside as perverts, while a number of others, who try hard to avoid being perverts (though according to their constitution they should be so regarded), are forced into nervous illness. It is not hard to foresee what will happen when sexual freedom is further restricted and the demands of civilization raised to the level of the third stage, at which all sexual activity outside marriage is condemned. The number of strong individuals who openly oppose the demands of civilization will increase to an extraordinary extent, and so will that of the less strong, who, caught between the pressures of civilization and the resistance of their constitution, take refuge in neurotic illness.

Let us try to answer the three questions that now arise:

(1) What task does the requirement of the third stage of civilization set the individual?

(2) Can the legitimate sexual satisfaction that it allows offer an acceptable compensation for the renunciation of all other satisfactions?

(3) In what relation do the possible harmful effects of this renunciation stand to its utilization in the cause of civilization?

The answer to the first question touches on a problem that has often been discussed and cannot be treated exhaustively here – that of sexual abstinence. What our third stage of civilization demands of the individual, whether man or woman, is premarital abstinence, and lifelong abstinence for all who do not enter into a lawful marriage. The assertion – which is acceptable to all authorities – that sexual abstinence is not harmful and not very hard to maintain has been widely endorsed by doctors. It may be said that the task of mastering such a powerful impulse as the sex drive otherwise than by satisfying it is one that can call for the whole of one's powers. Only a minority succeed in mastering it by sublimation, by directing the instinctual forces away from their sexual aim and towards higher cultural goals, and even this minority probably succeeds only for a time, and least easily during the period of ardent youthful vigour. Most of the rest become neurotic or are damaged in some other way. Experience shows that most of the people who make up our society are constitutionally not equal to abstinence. Whoever would have fallen ill under less severe sexual restrictions will do so more readily and more seriously under the demands of today's civilized sexual morality, for we know of no better safeguard against the threat posed to the normal sex drive by defective inherited dispositions and developmental disturbances than sexual satisfaction itself. The more someone is disposed to neurosis, the less able he is to endure abstinence; for the partial drives that have failed to develop normally, in the sense we have propounded, have at the same time become all the harder to inhibit. But many of those who would have retained their health under the requirements of the second stage of civilization are now exposed to neurosis. For the psychical value of sexual satisfaction increases when it is frustrated; the pent-up libido is now put in a position to seek out one or other of the weaker points in the structure of sexual life – which are seldom wanting – in order to

95

break through to a substitutive satisfaction of a neurotic kind, marked by pathological symptoms. Anyone qualified to investigate the conditioning factors of nervous illness will soon be convinced that the increase of nervous disorders in our society is due to the greater restrictions placed on sexual activity.

This brings us closer to the question of whether sexual intercourse in wedlock can fully compensate for its restriction before marriage. The evidence for a negative answer to this question is so abundant that we must confine ourselves to the briefest summary. We would above all remind the reader that our civilized sexual morality restricts sexual intercourse even within marriage by obliging married couples to content themselves, as a rule, with very few procreative acts. As a consequence of this consideration, satisfactory sexual intercourse in marriage takes place for only a few years – from which, of course, we should subtract those periods of abstention that are necessary for the protection of the wife's health. After these three, four or five years the marriage fails, in so far as it promised to satisfy the couple's sexual needs; for all the means of contraception that have been invented so far reduce sexual enjoyment, disturb the finer sensitivities of both partners, or are even direct causes of illness. Fear of the consequences of sexual intercourse is accompanied first by a diminution in the partners' physical tenderness, and then often in their spiritual affection for each other, which should have succeeded their original passionate love. In this state of mental disappointment and physical deprivation, which is thus the fate of most marriages, both partners find themselves back in the state they were in before they married, except that they are now bereft of an illusion, and once again have to rely on their fortitude in mastering and deflecting their sex drive. We will not inquire how well men succeed in this task in their maturer years; experience suggests that they quite often avail themselves of whatever freedom they are allowed, though only tacitly and reluctantly, by even the strictest sexual code. The 'double standard' that applies to the men in our society is the plainest admission that society itself, which has laid down the rules, does not believe it possible to comply with them. Experience tells us something about women too. As the true repositories of the sexual interests of humanity, they are only minimally endowed with the gift of sublimation and find the child at the breast, but not the growing child, a sufficient substitute for the sex object. When afflicted by marital disappointments, they fall prey to severe neuroses, which permanently darken their lives. Under today's cultural conditions marriage has long since ceased to be the panacea for women's nervous disorders; and even if we doctors continue to recommend it in such cases, we nevertheless know that a girl has to be fairly healthy in order to 'cope' with marriage, and we strongly advise our male patients against marrying girls who have had nervous trouble before marriage. The cure for the nervous illness that arises from marriage would instead be marital infidelity; however, the more strictly a woman has been brought up and the more seriously she has submitted to the requirements of civilization, the more afraid she is to take this way out, and in the conflict between her desires and her sense of duty she once again takes refuge in neurosis. Nothing protects her virtue as surely as sickness. The married state, which is held out as a consolation for the sex drive of civilized men and women in their youth, is thus unable to meet the requirements of the period of life that it occupies; there is no question of its compensating for earlier abstinence.

Even if it is conceded that such damage is caused by civilized sexual morality, it can still be argued, in answer to our third question, that what civilization gains from such an extreme sexual restriction probably more than balances these sufferings, which affect only a minority to any serious extent. I have to declare that in this matter I cannot properly balance gains against losses, but in assessing the losses I might put forward a number of other considerations. Going back to the question of abstinence, I have to say that it has other damaging effects apart from those pertaining to the neuroses, and that the importance of these neuroses is usually not fully appreciated.

The retardation of sexual development and sexual activity, which is the aim of our education and civilization, is certainly harmless at first; it is seen to be necessary when one considers the late age at which young people of the educated classes become independent and start to earn their living. Here, incidentally, one is reminded of how closely all our cultural institutions are interconnected and how difficult it is to change part of them without regard to the whole. However, abstinence that is prolonged much beyond the age of nineteen is no longer without its dangers for a young man and leads to harmful effects, even if not to nervous illness. True, it is said that the struggle with such a powerful drive and the emphasis that is necessarily placed on all the ethical and aesthetic forces in the mind 'steels' the character, and this is indeed true of some natures that enjoy a specially favourable constitution. It also has to be conceded that the differentiation of individual characters, which is so marked in our time, has become possible only with the imposition of sexual restrictions. In the great majority of cases, however, the struggle against sensuality uses up all the energy available to the character, and this at the very time when a young man needs all his forces if he is to win his rightful place in society. The relation between possible sublimation and necessary sexual activity naturally varies a good deal from individual to individual and even between different callings. An abstinent artist is almost inconceivable, but an abstinent young scholar is certainly no rarity. The latter can, through self-restraint, free the energy he needs for his studies, while the former's artistic achievements are probably greatly stimulated by his sexual experience. I do not in general have the impression that sexual abstinence helps produce energetic, independent men of action or original thinkers, bold liberators and reformers. Far more often it produces well-behaved weaklings who later merge into the great mass of those who habitually, if reluctantly, follow the lead given by strong individuals.

The fact that on the whole the sex drive behaves in a self-willed and unmanageable fashion is seen also in the results of efforts at abstinence. Civilized education, it is said, seeks to suppress it only temporarily, until marriage, intending then to set it free in order to make use of it. But extreme measures are more successful against the drive than attempts to moderate it. Very often suppression has gone too far, with the undesirable result that when the drive is set free it appears permanently impaired. Hence, total abstinence during youth is often not the best way to prepare a young man for marriage. Women sense this and prefer those of their suitors who have already proved their masculinity with other women. Especially obvious is the damage done to women's natures by the strict requirement of premarital abstinence. It is clear that education does not take lightly the task of suppressing a girl's sensuality until she marries, for it operates with the harshest means. Not only does it forbid sexual intercourse and put a high premium on the preservation of female innocence; it also shields the young woman from temptation as she matures, by keeping her in ignorance of any factual knowledge about the role she is destined for and by refusing to tolerate any amorous impulse that cannot lead to marriage. The result is that when the parental authorities suddenly allow girls to fall in love, they are psychically unequal to their new role and enter into marriage unsure of their own feelings. In consequence of the artificial retardation of their erotic function, they have nothing but disappointments to offer their husbands, who have saved up all their desire for them. Emotionally they are still attached to their parents, whose authority brought about the suppression of their sexuality, and in their physical behaviour they show themselves to be frigid, which prevents their husbands from experiencing any high degree of sexual enjoyment. I do not know whether the type of woman who is devoid of feeling and sensitivity exists in the absence of civilized education, but I think it probably does. In any case, education actually breeds it, and these women, who conceive without pleasure, subsequently show little readiness to face the pain of repeated childbirth. In this way, preparation for marriage frustrates the aims of marriage itself. Later, when the retardation of the wife's development is overcome and her full capacity for love awakens at the height of her existence as a woman, her relation with her husband has long since been ruined. As a reward for her earlier docility she is left with a choice between unsatisfied longing, infidelity and neurosis.

A person's sexual behaviour often *sets the pattern* for all his other ways of reacting to the world. Any man who energetically conquers his sex object is credited with the same ruthless energy in the pursuit of other goals too. Yet if, for a variety of reasons, he refrains from satisfying his strong sex drives, his behaviour in other spheres of life will be conciliatory and resigned, rather than energetic. A special application of the proposition that sexual life sets the pattern for the performance of other functions is easily seen in the female sex as a whole. Women's upbringing denies them the opportunity to take an intellectual interest in sexual problems, even though they have an extreme inherent curiosity, and frightens them by condemning such curiosity as unfeminine and the sign of a sinful disposition. In this way they are deterred from thinking at all, and knowledge loses its value for them. This prohibition on thought extends beyond the sexual sphere, partly owing to the unavoidable associations and partly automatically, in much the same way as when men are forbidden to think about religion or well-behaved subjects about loyalty. I do not believe that the biological opposition between intellectual work and sexual activity explains the 'physiological feeble-mindedness' of women, as Moebius has maintained in a controversial work. On the contrary, I think the undoubted intellectual inferiority of so many women can be traced back to the inhibition of thought that is essential for sexual suppression.

In considering the question of abstinence, an insufficiently strict distinction is made between two forms of it – abstention from all sexual activity and abstention from sexual intercourse with the opposite sex. Many of those who boast of their success in remaining abstinent have been able to do so only by recourse to masturbation and similar gratifications connected with the auto-erotic activities of early childhood. Yet precisely because of this link these substitutes for sexual satisfaction are by no means harmless; they dispose a person to the numerous forms of neurosis and psychosis that are conditional upon the reversion of the subject's sexual life to its infantile forms. Moreover, masturbation in no way meets the ideal requirements of civilized sexual morality and therefore drives young people into the very conflicts with the educational ideal that they sought to escape through abstinence. It also corrupts the character through *indulgence* in more ways than one: first, it teaches people to reach significant goals without expending any effort, by taking the easy route rather than committing all their energies to the task (that is, in accordance with the principle that *sexuality sets the pattern*); secondly, by raising the sexual object in the fantasies accompanying the satisfaction to a degree of excellence that is not easily rediscovered in reality. Hence, a witty writer, Karl Kraus, writing in the Viennese paper *Die Fackel*, was able to turn the truth on its head with the cynical remark that 'coition is only an inadequate surrogate for onanism'!

The stern demands of civilization and the difficult task of abstinence have combined to make avoidance of the union of the male and female genitals the essential feature of abstinence and to favour other forms of sexual activity that amount, one might say, to a kind of semi-obedience. Since normal sexual intercourse is so relentlessly persecuted on grounds of morality – and of hygiene too, in view of the possibilities of infection – the so-called perverse forms of heterosexual intercourse, in which other parts of the body take over the role of the genitals, have undoubtedly increased in social importance. Yet these activities cannot be judged to be as harmless as similar deviations in love relationships: they are ethically objectionable in that they degrade a love relationship between two human beings from something serious into a convenient game that entails no danger or spiritual involvement. As a further consequence of the difficulties to which normal sexual life has become subject, one must mention the spread of homosexual satisfaction; those whose homosexuality is due to their constitution or was acquired in childhood are now joined by many others, for whom, in their maturer years, the mainstream of the libido has been blocked off and the homosexual side-channel has consequently widened.

All these unavoidable and unintended consequences of the demand for abstinence combine to ensure that the preparation for marriage is thoroughly vitiated, despite the fact that, according to civilized sexual morality, marriage should be the sole heir to sexual strivings. All those men who, as a result of masturbatory or perverse practices, have oriented their libido to anything other than the normal situations and conditions of satisfaction, develop a diminished potency in marriage. And those women who have been able to preserve their virginity only with the help of similar means prove unresponsive to normal intercourse in marriage. A marriage that begins with a reduced capacity for love in both partners succumbs to the process of dissolution even more quickly than others. Thanks to the husband's limited potency, the wife is unsatisfied, and she herself remains devoid of feeling, even if her disposition to frigidity, deriving from her upbringing, might have been overcome by a powerful sexual experience. A couple like this will also find contraception more difficult than a healthy one, as the husband's reduced potency is not easily compatible with the use of contraceptives. At a loss for what to do, they will soon abandon sexual intercourse as the source of all their embarrassments, and with it the basis of married life.

I call upon all informed persons to confirm that I am not exaggerating, but simply describing conditions of which any number of equally bad examples can be observed. The uninitiated find it quite incredible that, among couples subject to our civilized sexual morality, normal potency is found so rarely in the husband and frigidity so often in the wife, that marriage involves such a degree of renunciation, often for both partners, and that married life, the happiness so fervently longed for, is reduced to so little. I have already shown how, under these conditions, the most obvious outcome is nervous illness; but I will add a word about the continued effect on the child or children – there are seldom more than one – who are born of such a marriage. At first sight we appear to have a case of hereditary transmission, but on closer inspection it is seen to be the result of powerful infantile impressions. In her role as a mother, a neurotic wife who is unsatisfied by her husband becomes over-affectionate and over-anxious towards her child, transfers to it her own need for love and thereby awakens it to sexual precocity. The poor understanding between the parents stimulates the child's emotional life and arouses in it, at a very tender age, intense feelings of love, hate and jealousy. A strict upbringing, which refuses to countenance any expression of sexuality, awakened so early, supplies the suppressive force, and this conflict, at this age, has all the makings of lifelong nervous illness.

I now revert to my earlier statement that assessments of neuroses usually fail to take account of their full significance. I am not referring to the underrating of these conditions that leads to their light-hearted dismissal by relatives or to assurances by self-important doctors that a few weeks of hydrotherapy or a few months' rest and convalescence will probably clear up the condition. These are simply the opinions of totally ignorant laymen and doctors – mostly just words, designed to offer the patients some short-term consolation. It is in fact well known that a chronic neurosis, even if it does not put an end to the patient's capacity to go on living, places a heavy burden on him, roughly comparable with that imposed by a tuberculosis or a cardiac defect. One might be prepared to accept this state of affairs if neurotic illness excluded only some of the weaker brethren from cultural activity, while allowing the rest to take part in it at the cost of merely subjective complaints. I would rather draw attention to the view that neurosis, whatever its extent and whoever is affected by it, is liable to frustrate the aims of civilization and thereby actually to promote the work of the suppressed mental forces opposed to it. Hence, if the price society pays for obedience to its extensive rules is an increase in nervous illness, it cannot register a gain bought at the cost of sacrifices, or indeed any gain at all. Let us consider, for instance, the frequent case of a woman who does not love her husband because she has no reason to – given the conditions under which she married him and her subsequent marital experience – but wishes she could do so, because this alone accords with the ideal of marriage to which she was brought up. She will suppress in herself any impulses that give expression to the truth and conflict with her loyalty to the ideal, and try hard to play the part of an affectionate, tender, attentive wife. Neurotic illness will result from this suppression of the self, and in a very short time it will have taken its toll on the unloved husband and produced in him just as much dissatisfaction and anxiety as would have resulted from an acknowledgement of the true state of affairs. This example is quite typical of what neurosis can lead to. A similar failure of compensation is to be observed after the suppression of other impulses that are inimical to civilization, but not directly sexual in character. For instance, anyone who has strenuously suppressed a constitutional tendency to harshness and cruelty and become *excessively kindly* is often so drained of energy that he cannot do everything that his compensatory impulses require, with the result that on the whole he does less good than he would have managed to do without suppressing his natural impulses.

Let us add that in general the restriction of sexual activity in a nation goes hand in hand with an increase in our anxiety about life and our fear of death, which impairs the capacity of individuals for enjoyment and puts an end to their readiness to embrace death for any purpose, which results in a diminished inclination to procreate children and excludes the nation or the group in question from any share in the future. If this is so, we may well ask whether our 'civilized' sexual morality is worth the sacrifices it forces on us, especially if we have not yet sufficiently freed ourselves from hedonism to be able to resist including a modicum of individual happiness among the aims of our cultural development. It is certainly not for the physician to come forward with proposals for reform, but I think I might emphasize the urgency of such proposals if I supplement Ehrenfels's description of the harmful effects of our 'civilized' sexual morality by pointing to its significant role in the spread of modern nervous illness.

(1908)

Notes

1. L. Löwenfeld (ed.), *Grenzfragen des Nerven- und Seelenlebens*, LVI, Wiesbaden 1907.
2. *Sexualethik*, p. 32ff.
3. Op. cit., p. 35.
4. *Über die wachsende Nervosität unserer Zeit*, [Heidelberg] 1893.
5. *Die Pathologie und Therapie der Neurasthenie*, [Jena] 1896.
6. *Nervosität und neurasthenische Zustände*, [Vienna] 1895, p. 11. (In Nothnagel's *Handbuch der spez. Pathologie und Therapie*.)
7. *Sammlung kleiner Schriften zur Neurosenlehre*, Vienna 1906 (4th impression 1922) (*Gesammelte Werke*, vol. I).
8. [Here Freud uses the English word.]
9. *Drei Abhandlungen zur Sexualtheorie* [*Three Essays on the Theory of Sexuality*], Vienna 1905 [II.6] (*Gesammelte Werke*, vol. V).

READ MORE IN PENGUIN

In every corner of the world, on every subject under the sun, Penguin represents quality and variety – the very best in publishing today.

For complete information about books available from Penguin – including Puffins, Penguin Classics and Arkana – and how to order them, write to us at the appropriate address below. Please note that for copyright reasons the selection of books varies from country to country.

In the United Kingdom: Please write to *Dept. EP, Penguin Books Ltd, Bath Road, Harmondsworth, West Drayton, Middlesex UB7 0DA*

In the United States: Please write to *Consumer Services, Penguin Putnam Inc., 405 Murray Hill Parkway, East Rutherford, New Jersey 07073-2136.* VISA and MasterCard holders call 1-800-631-8571 to order Penguin titles

In Canada: Please write to *Penguin Books Canada Ltd, 10 Alcorn Avenue, Suite 300, Toronto, Ontario M4V 3B2*

In Australia: Please write to *Penguin Books Australia Ltd, 487 Maroondah Highway, Ringwood, Victoria 3134*

In New Zealand: Please write to *Penguin Books (NZ) Ltd, Private Bag 102902, North Shore Mail Centre, Auckland 10*

In India: Please write to *Penguin Books India Pvt Ltd, 11 Community Centre, Panchsheel Park, New Delhi 110017*

In the Netherlands: Please write to *Penguin Books Netherlands bv, Postbus 3507, NL-1001 AH Amsterdam*

In Germany: Please write to *Penguin Books Deutschland GmbH, Metzlerstrasse 26, 60594 Frankfurt am Main*

In Spain: Please write to *Penguin Books S. A., Bravo Murillo 19, 1°B, 28015 Madrid*

In Italy: Please write to *Penguin Italia s.r.l., Via Vittorio Emanuele 45/a, 20094 Corsico, Milano*

In France: Please write to *Penguin France, 12, Rue Prosper Ferradou, 31700 Blagnac*

In Japan: Please write to *Penguin Books Japan Ltd, Iidabashi KM-Bldg, 2-23-9 Koraku, Bunkyo-Ku, Tokyo 112-0004*

In South Africa: Please write to *Penguin Books South Africa (Pty) Ltd, P.O. Box 751093, Gardenview, 2047 Johannesburg*

THE NEW PENGUIN FREUD

The Psychopathology of Everyday Life
Translated by Anthea Bell
Introduction by Paul Keegan

'A modernist . . . playing with meaning, creating a new language for the idea of self' – *Independent*

The most trivial slips of the tongue or pen, Freud believed, can reveal our secret ambitions, money worries and sexual fantasies.

The Psychopathology of Everyday Life ranks among his most entertaining and accessible works. Starting with the story of how he once forgot the name of an Italian painter – and how a young acquaintance mangled a quotation from Virgil through fears that his girlfriend might be pregnant – it brings together a treasure trove of muddled memories, inadvertent actions and verbal tangles. Amusing, moving and deeply revealing of the repressed, hypocritical Viennese society of his day, Freud's dazzling interpretations provide the perfect introduction to psychoanalytic thinking in action.

THE NEW PENGUIN FREUD

The Schreber Case

Translated by Andrew Webber
Introduction by Colin MacCabe

'The memoirs of Schreber and Freud's analysis of them . . .
still speak to our most abiding problems' – Colin MacCabe

Freud rarely treated psychotic patients (or, indeed,
psychoanalysed people from their writings), but he had a
powerful and imaginative understanding of their condition –
revealed, most notably, in this analysis of a remarkable
memoir.

In 1903, Judge Daniel Paul Schreber, a highly intelligent and
cultured man, produced a vivid account of a nervous illness
dominated by the desire to become a woman, terrifying
delusions about his doctor and a belief in his own special
relationship with God. Eight years later, Freud's penetrating
insight uncovered the unacceptable impulses and feelings
Schreber had about his father, which underlay his
extravagant symptoms. Yet he also demonstrated the link
with more normal patterns of psychosexual development –
and the human tendency to transform love into hate.

Wild Analysis

Translated by Alan Bance
Introduction by Adam Phillips

This powerful volume brings together Freud's most
significant writings on psychoanalytic method and the
question of psychoanalytic technique.

The fundamental concern of these works is the complex
relationship between patient and analyst. Here Freud
explores both the crucial importance of and the huge risks
involved in patients' transference of their emotions onto
their therapist. He also shows the ambiguous dangers of
'wild analysis' by doctors who are insufficiently trained or
offer instant solutions; looks at issues such as the length
of a treatment; and offers a trenchant discussion of the
controversy surrounding psychoanalysis as a medical
discipline. And, in examining the tensions between the
practice of psychoanalysis and its central theory – the
disruptive nature of the unconscious – Freud asks, can
there ever really be rules for analysis?

THE NEW PENGUIN FREUD

The 'Wolfman' and Other Cases

Translated by Louise Adey Huish
Introduction by Gillian Beer

When a disturbed young Russian man came to Freud for treatment, the analysis of his childhood neuroses – most notably a dream about wolves outside his bedroom window – eventually revealed a deep-seated trauma. It took over four years to treat him and the 'Wolfman' became Freud's most famous case.

This volume also contains the case history of five-year-old 'Little Hans's' fear of horses; the 'Ratman's' violent fears of rats gnawing into his father and lover; and the essay 'Some Character Types', in which Freud draws on the work of Shakespeare, Ibsen and Nietzsche to demonstrate different kinds of resistance to therapy. Above all, the case histories show us Freud at work, in his own words.

THE NEW PENGUIN FREUD

The Joke and Its Relation to the Unconscious

Translated by Joyce Crick
Introduction by John Carey

Why do we laugh? The answer, argued Freud in this
groundbreaking study of humour, is that jokes, like dreams,
satisfy our unconscious desires.

The Joke and Its Relation to the Unconscious (1905) explains
how jokes provide immense pleasure by releasing us from
our inhibitions and allowing us to express sexual, aggressive,
playful or cynical instincts that would otherwise remain
hidden. In elaborating this theory, Freud brings together a
rich collection of puns, witticisms, one-liners and anecdotes,
many of which throw a vivid light on the society of early
twentieth-century Vienna. Jokes, as Freud shows, are a way
of giving ourselves away.

FORTHCOMING FREUD TITLES
IN PENGUIN MODERN CLASSICS

The Psychology of Love
Translated by Joyce Crick
Introduced by John Carey

The Future of an Illusion
Translated by Jim Underwood
Introduced by Jacqueline Rose

Leonardo da Vinci and a Memory of His Childhood
Translated by David McLintock
Introduced by Hugh Haughton

An Outline of Psychoanalysis
Translated by Helena Ragg-Kirkby
Introduced by Malcolm Bowie

Beyond the Pleasure Principle
Translated by John Reddick
Introduced by Mark Edmunson

The Unconscious
Translated by Graham Frankland
Introduced by James Conant

Mourning and Melancholia
Translated by Shaun Whiteside
Introduced by Maud Ellman

Studies in Hysteria
Translated by Nicola Luckhurst
Introduced by Rachael Bowlby

The Interpretation of Dreams
Translated by Jim Underwood
Introduced by John Forrester